PROTECTING CHILDREN THROUGH DIVORCE

Building Healthy Pathways

PROTECTING CHILDREN THROUGH DIVORCE

12 Self-Guided Reflections

CHRISTINA MARIE CALDERWOOD

PROTECTING CHILDREN THROUGH DIVORCE
BUILDING HEALTHY PATHWAYS
BY CHRISTINA MARIE CALDERWOOD

First Edition
Copyright © 2025 by Christina Marie Calderwood

Published by
Munn Avenue Press
300 Main Street, Ste 21
Madison, NJ 07940
MunnAvenuePress.com

For permission requests, contact MunnAvenuePress.com

Paperback ISBN: 978-1-969679-09-4
Hardcover ISBN: 978-1-969679-10-0

Printed in the United States of America

This book is dedicated to
the children whose strength and
resilience inspired this journey.

Contents

Preface

I GREW UP in a loving, traditional household. It wasn't perfect, but it gave me a strong sense of stability. What I remember most are the small things that made me feel safe: the Sunday roast dinners, the smell of my grand- mother's cigarettes, the way my mom's perfume lingered in the kitchen. That house gave me a sense of calm and predictability. Even with all its imperfections, it always felt like home.

My parents were blue-collar workers, firmly lower-mid- dle class. My Italian mother grew up on a farm, shaped by strict traditional values. She was mostly a stay-at-home mom but took retail jobs when times were tight. My father worked long hours in a hot factory, machining flooring to keep food on the table. Christmases felt magical, not from abundance but because my parents poured everything they had into making sure we had more than enough under the tree. On Christmas mornings in our long, ranch-style house, we would come out of our bedrooms and walk down the hallway toward the living room, which was filled with gifts. I can still picture my father smiling from his recliner, knowing how much he had poured into making that joy possible.

I have one brother, Michael, younger than me, who has a loving wife and two beautiful children. We weren't especially close growing up. We had the usual mix of love and conflict that siblings typically share, but one thing was always clear: we were deeply loved, and he was my little brother. As adults, with both of us going through difficult times in our lives, we did lots of healing work through self-reflection and have grown incredibly close now that we have found more in common. Today, we talk all the time, enjoying a relationship I'm deeply grateful for. It reminds me that healing is possible, even though our early years were distant. He lives out of state, but we make it a point to see each other every year.

Recently, we met as a family in Hawaii to watch my brother and his wife renew their vows on the beach after 25 years of marriage. My mom, my husband, my daughter, my niece, and my nephew were there. It was a very special trip for all of us. As I write this book, we are planning to pick my brother and his wife up from the airport, as they are coming for a visit. I am excited to just hang out with him for a few days. We have some of the deepest talks together, often reminiscing about times we have shared that we both feel grateful for.

Growing up, our weekends meant card games with family and friends, and laughter spilling from the kitchen as my parents played cribbage, cigarettes burning slowly, my grandfather's spittoon nearby. Sundays were sacred. Every week, we had roast beef with mashed potatoes dripping in butter. Family vacations were rare but incredibly special: trips to Disney World, Polar Caves, and Santa's Village felt enormous precisely because they were rare, cherished moments.

Life in our home followed a comforting pattern. It wasn't about luxury or excitement, it was about anticipation, about knowing what to expect, about the quiet security of family. Make no mistake, our family certainly had its flaws. It wasn't all June Cleaver and Mike Brady (some of you might have to Google those names!) We had our hard times too—fighting, yelling, often disciplined too strongly as our parents were influenced by old-fashioned ways. Those rhythms certainly shaped who I am today, some of it good and some of it requiring me to work hard to overcome.

Movies were only shown annually back then, with no DVR, Cable TV, or Firesticks. We had to wait; there was no instant gratification. I remember the two times per year we shared the most special family time, watching *Willy Wonka* and *The Wizard of Oz*. My mom would work us up for more than a month with anticipation and excitement. She would get us our favorite candy as a treat, make popcorn, and buy soda. It was so special, and something to look forward to. We used to go to the local drive-in movies a time or two in the summer. Mom would pack us special snacks, the ones we couldn't afford on the regular. Dad would open the back of the station wagon, lay out blankets and pillows for my brother and me, and we'd watch the movie while eating our special snacks. I can recall for certain that we saw the original *Bambi* and *Dumbo*. Such wonderful memories!

I was raised Catholic, faithfully attending Sunday school, moving through all the sacraments, and marrying in a Catholic church. Over time, my faith has shifted into something quieter and more personal, but no less profound.

College wasn't financially possible for me, so at 18, I put on a suit and drove from office building to office building until I landed an entry-level accounting job. For 26 years, I climbed the corporate ladder, eventually reaching director-level positions. Yet despite my success, something was always missing. I felt disconnected. Finance didn't align with my deep desire to help people. About 15 years into my career, when I was working in international finance, I spent about 80% of each month traveling globally to sort out how we would get paid for deals our sales team had closed. In a hotel room in Colombia, I thought, *This isn't for me.*

Unfortunately, I was stuck. We were in the heat of building our home, and our daughter Nichole was about 12 or 13. How could I possibly consider a new career? Finance was all I knew, and we needed my income to keep pressing toward our goals. I stayed in it until I took a position in administration at a forensic psychiatric hospital. Finally, I felt like I was fulfilling my purpose, not to crunch numbers but to help those in need. From the day I took that job in 2018, I have felt complete in my career. Every day, I continue to work toward growth and to serve.

I remember sitting in my office, staring at spreadsheets and thinking, *This can't be it; there must be more.* That quiet nudge would ultimately lead me somewhere entirely new.

By 40, I realized that if I wanted my life to change, I needed a degree. The thought of going back to school terrified me . . . what if I was too old, too far behind, too out of place? Despite my fears, I took out loans and enrolled anyway.

Earning first my bachelor's and then my master's became more than academic goals. They helped me reclaim who I was meant to be. That decision changed everything. It allowed me to finally embrace my true calling: helping others.

In the years that followed, that calling would lead me down an unexpected path from finance to hospital administration, recovery coaching, holistic nutrition, wellness coaching, and eventually becoming a licensed counselor.

However, back then, I was just beginning to find my way.

I met Scott when I was sixteen, and we married when I was twenty. At the time, it felt secure. We had the kind of commitment my parents had shown me. Looking back,

I see how young we were. We had our daughter Nichole when I was just twenty, and she remains the greatest gift of my life. I threw myself into motherhood, attending every cheer competition, karate tournament, and softball game. I have zero regrets. As you might suspect, somewhere along the way, I lost sight of myself. I didn't realize how much I'd sacrificed until Nichole got a bit older and started gaining independence. It's a story many mothers know well. How easily we lose ourselves in caring for everyone else. It may sound cliché, but it's a common truth in the world I live in.

That's when I truly began to see how different Scott and I had become. It is a story many can relate to. Two very young kids thrown into the very adult world of having a child, working toward the American dream of a nice home, nice vehicles, vacations, and providing a lucrative life. We threw ourselves into it all. We built and sold three homes together and moved often, continuing to invest and grow financially. Somewhere along the way, we got lost in the race and lost track of each other.

We knew we had to tell Nichole we were separating, but we never felt ready. One day, I suggested that Scott and I step out of our house and into neutral territory: the parking lot behind a local pizza place. We both broke down, hyperventilating, crying, and saying over and over, "She's going to fall apart." Gently, we consoled each other. "Not today. Just breathe . . .."

Inside, I barely held it together. It felt like something was breaking in me. *We're not going to break her. We're going to protect her.* For over an hour, we sat together in pain, trying to form a plan rooted in love and unity. I don't think either of us could fully process the reality of divorce. For me, it felt like the worst emotional hurricane I would ever face.

I honestly don't remember if I have this right, and were I to ask Scott or Nichole, their version might be entirely different. I think it was a Saturday morning, at the familiar kitchen counter. We said, "We've decided we're not going to be married anymore." I remember that Nichole went quiet, then began to cry, in big, silent tears.

Her questions came quickly. "Are we still going to live here?" "Do I have to choose?"

We reassured her, "You'll always have both of us. This isn't about taking anything away."

We held her as she cried, wishing we could carry all her pain for her. In that moment, it felt like the beautiful castle we had built was crumbling brick by brick. One thing was certain—we were determined to hold it together. For her. Our grief could wait; her safety came first.

We remained consistent, united in our love for her. In the background, I carried a quiet fear that the pain of our separation might break one of us or all of us. Our separation affected us all, including those closest to us. Everywhere I turned, people asked, "What happened? You seemed so happy. Why did you leave?" The doubt was overwhelming. It was the scariest time of my life, filled with uncertainty. We kept fighting through it all. We showed up at events, competitions, and games. We offered kindness even when it felt impossible. Our commitment to protect Nichole's emotional space guided us through years of careful rebuilding. As our blended family began to form, it felt awkward at first and for quite some time after.

A few years later, I was at work when my boyfriend Mike called to say hello. He mentioned that he and Scott were meeting for breakfast and taking the motorcycles out. I paused, trying to take it in. My boyfriend and ex-husband were going for a ride together. It caught me off guard, but beneath the strangeness was a quiet reassurance. Maybe, just maybe, this was the beginning of real healing. It wasn't something I expected, but I deeply needed it. Maybe all those fears that we would never move forward were finally beginning to ease. Today, Scott and I are both remarried. Nichole lovingly calls our new spouses her *bonus mom and bonus dad*. Our blended family, built on compassion and care, is something that amazes me every day.

When our separation became public, the judgment came swiftly. Some people withdrew, while others looked at me differently. I felt exposed, as if my life was on display. I wasn't just grieving my marriage; I was grieving the loss of people I thought would stand by me. I got so sick of people making a beeline for me at the local Walmart. People who would have normally avoided even saying hello. We lived in a small town where everyone knew everything, and this was no exception. Everyone wanted the story.

People would come up to me and say, "Hi, Christina. My goodness, what happened with you and Scott? We heard the news. So sorry."

It was exhausting. I felt like taking out an ad in the local paper with all the details, just to get it over with. It wore me down.

My hope in sharing my story isn't to offer a perfect road-map. It's to offer a reflection of possibility. Divorce doesn't have to be destructive. With intention, self-regulation, and relentless love, families can evolve and remain whole, even when their structure changes. There will always be unsafe situations beyond our control, but in most divorces, children deserve to maintain as much normalcy as possible, sharing a bond with both of the parents they so deeply love, and without adult emotions getting in the way.

I'm not an expert. I'm just a woman who lived through one of the hardest chapters of her life and came out more whole on the other side. Everything I share comes from my life, my opinion, and my personal experience. I believe our divorce story is unique because we chose to do it differently. We used one attorney, drove to court together, and focused on protecting our daughter every step of the way. It wasn't easy. It was the hardest thing we've ever done. Thankfully, in the end, the outcome has brought us all together.

This book isn't here to tell you what to do; it's here to sit beside you. It is to remind you that even when everything feels like it's falling apart, there's a way forward that puts your child's well-being at the center while honoring your growth.

For many years now, I have dreamed about telling our story with the hope that it would help others. While our divorce journey was tremendously sad and difficult, the blended family it gave us is something I will be eternally grateful for. You picked up this book, and that tells me you're trying. Trying is everything.

xo,

Christina

Introduction

I BELIEVE YOU picked up this book because you're look-ing for a way to do this differently—with more care, more intention, and more stability for your children. You might be searching for a new way forward. You could be deep in the process, trying to figure out what comes next. Or maybe you're holding out hope for the happiest possible ending. Whatever brought you here, I want to thank you for turning the pages. My hope is that by sharing our story, I can help guide you through your own.

This isn't just my story, it's a space for yours too. I invite you to walk alongside me, pause where you need to, and reflect as you go. Choose a journal that resonates with you: hardcover, softcover, leather, digital. Whatever works for you, speaks to you. Grab your favorite pen or pencil and let this process become yours. You deserve a space to be honest with yourself. *This isn't the typical book you pick up and read until you finish.* This isn't the kind of book you read straight through. It's one you can come back to. Pause, re-read, reflect, and keep it close when you need it. Maybe you'll pick it up again one day and look back at how far you've come. Maybe your challenges will continue for a while, and you'll keep journaling in new ways as the days, weeks, and months pass. Wherever you are, be present in the moment and continue to reflect.

Throughout this book, I'll share what happened in my life and how I moved through it, one step at a time. You'll also find space in each reflection to process your own experiences. Each reflection invites you to engage in a way that is personal and meaningful. *This is not a textbook, it's a conversation.* It's a place to lay things down and shape your thoughts. A place to be real with yourself.

Divorce is never easy. Whether it's been bittersweet, heartbreaking, or just plain confusing, what you do next matters, not only for yourself, but for your children. The choices you make shape their future, no matter what age they are. The pressure of this can feel overwhelming, but it can also be empowering. This is your chance to create something steady and loving, even when everything else feels uncertain.

This book is not a blueprint. It's a guide shaped by lived experience: messy, honest, and real. The reflections you'll find here are drawn from the hardest parts of my journey. The prompts are here to help you clear your energy so you can truly reflect. By the end, I hope you won't just have read about my healing, but will start walking toward yours.

Maybe you will even create your own reflections based on your personal experience.

Each of the twelve reflections includes:

- A short story from my life
- A self-care reminder to keep you grounded
- Questions to help you center your child's needs
- Journal prompts

None of the reflections need to be read in order. We all know life doesn't work that way, and neither does healing. Some reflections will land right away. Others you can return to when the time is right. That's okay. Come back when you're ready. If you find yourself revisiting a chapter more than once, take that as a sign of growth, not failure. If you have already experienced a reflection, take some time to journal about it.

At the start of each reflection, you'll find practical, grounding prompts. Sometimes, self-care is asking for help. Sometimes it's giving yourself permission to cry in the car before going back inside. Sometimes it's putting your phone down instead of sending that message. These small acts matter. They remind your nervous system that you're safe, that you're still in charge, that you're going to be okay.

Each reflection is different. Some may ask you to ground yourself in the present moment, while others suggest a few minutes of breath work, a gentle stretch, or a brief walk. These prompts are designed to help you clear your mind, focus, and approach the reflection with a calm and mindful perspective. Find what makes you personally feel grounded; we are all unique. They are simply suggestions, so do what feels best to you.

At the end of each reflection, you'll see a Journal Moment. This is a chance to pause, reflect, and explore your thoughts before moving forward. However, don't hesitate to stop anywhere along the way and journal when your thoughts take you there. Ask yourself: Where am I with this topic? What do I need right now to feel calm and grounded? What's one small choice I can make today that supports my child's emotional well-being, and supports my own? If it's something you haven't encountered yet, take a moment to prepare emotionally. You don't need perfect answers, only presence and intention.

Maybe a reflection will trigger an unrelated discussion you want to journal. This is your journey. *There are no right or wrong answers.*

In the early days of my divorce, I didn't know how we were going to make it through. I had to keep parenting while managing grief, money, meals, housing, paperwork, silence, and moments of complete exhaustion. There were times I responded calmly, and times I didn't. I kept showing up. I showed up when it was uncomfortable, when it was easier not to, when I had to dig deep and trust that it mattered. *That's how healing works. Not all at once, but moment by moment.*

You may have a supportive co-parent. You might be

dealing with stonewalling, conflict, sabotage, or unpredictability. I've been there too. The early years of our divorce were far from easy. No matter your personal situation, keeping things steady for the kids matters more than anything.

Even small acts of staying steady became my strength. Even if you're the only one showing up with love, clarity, and care, it all matters. Your children feel it; they will remember it.

You and your former partner may not always agree. However, there's one place where unity matters most, and that's the message your children receive. That message should be clear and unwavering: *You are safe. You are loved. WE are still your parents.* Even if the adults are struggling behind the scenes, that front-facing message matters more than you can imagine.

This book is for parents who want to move forward with integrity. It's for people ready to break the cycle of bitterness and blame, striving for something healthier for themselves and their children. Whether you're in a high-conflict situation, a low-contact arrangement, a peaceful separation, or somewhere in between, there is space here for all of it.

There are so many benefits to self-reflecting: gaining clarity, understanding yourself more deeply, creating space for personal growth, transforming blame into learning, and developing confidence, values, and boundaries.

On the contrary, please be mindful of self-judgment, negative thoughts, and feelings of self-sabotage. Try not to turn reflection into self-criticism. Be gentle with yourself. If you start to feel anxious at any time, take a break and practice some redirection, turning negative thoughts into compassionate thoughts. Always be mindful that self-reflecting can surface emotions that can be difficult to face. Identify your coping mechanisms and be ready for these moments so you can show yourself compassion and understanding. Treat yourself with love and kindness.

What I've learned is this: You don't have to be fully healed to be a good parent. You just need to be aware of what you're carrying, and willing to do the work to lay some of it down.

Take this at your pace. Come back to it when you need to. Skip ahead, pause, scribble in the margins. *This book is yours now.* You won't get everything right. Even so, if you show up with care, that's what your children will remember.

You're not alone in this. Let's begin.

Reflection One:
You've Decided to Tell
the Children

PROMPT 1

Before starting this reflection, take a moment to relax in a way that feels right for you. You might try breathwork, yoga, meditation, a warm bath, or a quiet cup of tea. Maybe going for a run clears your mind, or lighting candles helps you feel grounded. Find what grounds you. Is your journal ready? Do you have your favorite pen? When you feel prepared to explore your thoughts and emotions, let's take this journey together.

BREAKING THE NEWS to your child that you're separating or divorcing is one of the most vulnerable and emotional things a parent may ever do. It's also one of the most important. The words we choose, the tone we use, our body language, and the emotional environment we create in those moments all matter. They become part of our child's internal story forever.

Your child absorbs it all: your words, your body language, even the emotions you try to hide. They don't just hear what you say, they feel who you are. Children notice more than we think and at all ages. So, take your time. Plan gently, lead with as much calm and love as you can gather.

This reflection is shared with the intention of helping you feel less alone as you prepare for that conversation. It doesn't offer perfection, just one parent's experience of choosing honesty, co-regulation, and deep emotional care during one of life's hardest transitions. We certainly didn't do it all perfectly, hence the reason I can share so much with you now. Remember, it is not about perfection, it's about being mindful of the damage adult emotions can cause a child.

You may be taking this journey on your own, despite how much you want both of you to be there. I believe it is easier to feel empathy than hatred. Stay with what YOU are going to do for the children. We had to keep showing up for Nichole, even when it felt impossible to be there. We tried to approach each moment with as much mindfulness as we could, because we knew it would stay with her. I want to share how we planned to tell our daughter Nichole, because that moment shaped everything that followed. While I cannot remember the exact details of it all, I do remember that Scott and I planned to deliver a united, confusion-free message to her that would allow her to feel as safe as possible in such a trying situation.

MY STORY: HOW WE TOLD NICHOLE

Before and during our divorce, we watched other families navigate their separations. We saw the emotional impact it had on their children—often unintended, but real. Many of those children ended up holding emotional burdens that didn't belong to them. Watching that unfold, I kept thinking, *Dear God, I don't want our daughter to suffer like that.*

It became a quiet promise to ourselves: we love our daughter; we are not going to do this to her.

Nichole was fifteen, nearing sixteen. I imagine she already knew something was shifting since we might have appeared different for a while. We chose to sit down together to tell her, with the clearest message we could offer: "We've decided to divorce, but this is not your fault; you are deeply loved." We told her she wouldn't lose either of us and we meant it. I don't remember exactly what we said that day, but I'm sure she does. Moments like that stay with a child. Every word, every pause, every expression . . . they never forget.

Telling her is a blur to me now. I wish I had kept a journal during that time, something like the one you're writing in now. As hard as it would have been, it might help me remember how far we've come. What I do remember is her crying and the look on her face. Absorbing that pain, seeing it on her face, was unbearable. Of course, she was sad. How could this not be difficult news, no matter how we said it?

As prepared as you might think you are, this news is still

From left to right: Our son-in-law, our daughter, my mom & dad, Scott & Tina, me and my bonus son and our beautiful golden Madaket- 2023

going to hurt your child. Nichole had likely seen enough to know something was coming, but that didn't shield her from the heartache.

When we told her, I saw it all over her face. She was trying so hard to be strong, but the sadness ran deep. To see that kind of sorrow in the person I loved most in this world, knowing that we were the cause of it, was overwhelming. I think that's why I can't remember the details now. The intensity of it all was too much, and my mind simply closed the door.

It's heartbreaking to witness your child in that kind of pain. In any case, we were ready in one way that mattered: our message was united. Words alone weren't enough. Over time, it was our consistency that built her trust back up.

That old phrase, "Actions speak louder than words," couldn't have been truer. We said she could trust us, and then we kept showing up to prove it.

Over time, she came to believe us. Not because of one conversation but because of what we did afterward. She saw both of us there, again and again. That's how trust was rebuilt. She had questions, of course. *Why is this happening? Is it my fault? Are we still a family?* We let her ask and we answered. We didn't answer with complicated explanations, but with honesty, warmth, and reassurance.

What mattered most was making space for her feelings. We didn't rush her through them or try to fix them. We just stayed present. We were always mindful of what we said in front of her, even when our own emotions weren't aligned or easy to manage. Some of those feelings were painful or dark, but they weren't hers to carry.

The hardest part for many parents is managing their grief without letting it spill into their child's world. Our children need to feel our steadiness, not our chaos. That's the boundary, that's the work.

Internally, I was holding so much: fear, sadness, and guilt. There were moments when the emotions felt heavier than I could carry. I processed privately in journals, in silence, on long walks where I let the feelings come without reacting to them. It helped me regulate so I could be present for Nichole.

There was pain in our community, too. We faced judgment. Some people didn't understand why I left. I thought certain friendships were unconditional. When they shifted, it hurt deeply.

Over time, though, I began to see that the only thing I could control was how I responded. That realization helped me reclaim power. I learned to let go of resentment by reminding myself that they just didn't understand. I chose not to hold hate. I practiced forgiveness, not to excuse but to heal. A close friend called me one day and tore into me. She was downright mean! She screamed at me on the phone, "You had it all; what is wrong with you?" In the beginning, I would yell back and shut the conversation down. Then I'd hang up and feel sick about it. Or at least say, "Screw you!"

At that point, I turned my feelings around to a more forgiving outlook. Rather than responding unfavourably, I began to say things like, "I know it seemed like we had it all, but sadly, something broke. Unfortunately, we didn't make it through but we are all going to be okay. Thank you for asking." I realized quickly that lashing out was hurting me the most, and I was already in enough pain.

Eventually, many of those friendships returned—some in new forms, others stronger than before. I started to notice that when I shifted the energy I was putting out, when I gave what I hoped to receive, it began to come back.

Scott and I had different emotional paths, but we were both hurting so much. Through it all, we stayed aligned on one thing: Nichole was our priority. That intention grounded us. Even at our worst moments, we reminded ourselves that how we handled this would shape how she came through it.

There were hard times. Shared spaces like sporting events were painful, but we kept going. We reminded each other that this wasn't about us. She didn't need to carry our pain. Her only job was to be herself. We knew that our actions, not just our words, would shape how she got through it. Our responsibility was to create the safety and stability for her to do that.

No, it wasn't easy; we were both quietly sinking. Still, we didn't hand her our emotional weight. That was our work to hold. That's what selflessness looked like in this context. Not perfection, but the daily choice to protect her emotional space.

I remember a specific moment when Nichole and her college roommate were looking for their next apartment for the upcoming year. Scott and I continued to struggle through. We talked on the phone and the conversations were not going well. I felt worried because in that moment, I thought about how to support Nichole in this wonderful experience she was embarking on, but I wondered how Scott and I could pull it together. Scott and I agreed we would meet at her college that Saturday morning to look at the few places that she and her roommate had narrowed down. When we arrived, my stomach was turning and I couldn't eat without getting sick. Nichole and her room-mate were waiting for us. Nichole told us a story and I felt so proud of her; it took all the focus off of what Scott and I were going through for that moment. It helped me put into perspective that no matter our struggles, our daughter was still moving in a healthy direction.

Days before, she and her roommate rode around with the realtor, looking at lots of places. She said, "Mom, we were driving in the area, and I asked the realtor, 'Do you have kids of your own?' He shared that he did. I asked him if he would want them to live in this area, because it didn't look very safe.' He said 'No, I guess not,' and I said, 'Great, why don't you focus on showing us areas you would want your own children to live in?'"

That's our girl! we thought. She found a beautiful place, and we were so proud. Scott and I stood together in their new apartment, united and smiling with pride, forgetting about the previous hours of complete agony. When our focus remained on Nichole, our love for her somehow overthrew the pain.

For a long time, divorce didn't feel like an option. I kept trying to fix things. I believed I could. I told myself I had to. That I was failing by leaving.

When I finally saw the reality that I wasn't stopping this, I felt like everything collapsed. I remember thinking, *This is really happening. I don't know how to do this. What happens to our home? To Nichole? To Scott?*

Once I accepted that it was happening, something shifted. My focus changed. I stopped asking how to stop it and began asking: How do I help us get through this?

There was no space for a breakdown, so I had to stay steady. Not for me, but for Nichole. Scott and I would eventually heal, but she didn't get to walk away from the pain. We had to help her through it.

That became the guiding principle: *This isn't about me. This isn't about Scott. This is about her.*

It wasn't about shielding her from pain, because that's not possible. It was about showing her that even when life hurts, love stays. Even when everything breaks, kindness can still hold. That took a great deal of trust rebuilding, and we worked hard on it for many years to follow.

We told her we were getting a divorce after we had processed as much of our own pain as we could. We chose to tell her selflessly. Not to offload, but to reassure.

One of our friends had to tell his kids alone. He knew that their mom would blame, shame, and not be able to hold it together. He made this decision so he could console them and try to protect them from the agony of adult feelings. Not everyone is going to be able to tell the children together, in a united manner. Not every situation will continue in a healthy direction, as in the case of my friend, where the mom continued down this path for many years to follow. He persevered in what most would call "damage control," constantly redirecting and supporting the children in every possible way. Since you are here, I believe you want to be a parent who continues down the pathway of protecting your children. No matter your situation, you can help your children through the pain of your divorce with self-control and mindfulness.

Nichole trusted us over time because we were consistent and we kept showing up. We never asked her to carry the heaviness that we were still learning to manage ourselves.

We were committed to doing this well, not because it was easy but because she deserved it.

Watching other families helped us learn what not to do. That quiet promise to protect Nichole became how we made every decision. Even when we didn't know if we were succeeding, we kept going. We stayed determined to be kind, to be respectful.

Somehow, through all of it, we stayed kind to each other, and through more and more evolving, we stayed friends.

There were moments over the years that reminded us how far we'd come. School events, birthdays, even shared holidays—times that could have been tense but weren't. We learned to sit beside each other in support of Nichole, to cheer her on together even when our hearts were still mending in different ways. We went from the ends of the bench, back to the middle, together but in a different way.

It took time; it took months, even years to feel like we had found our rhythm. The more we chose peace, the more secure she became. Co-parenting eventually became about building something steady and real. It became our life-long commitment again, something we could shift our focus back to. In many ways, co-parenting supported our journey into healing.

Did we do everything perfectly? No. Are we experts? Definitely not. You won't be either, and that's okay. What matters is effort, care, and consistency. We tried our best to support Nichole through one of the most chaotic times in our lives, staying united so she wouldn't have to guess where she stood.

In hindsight, I do wish we'd gone to family therapy. Nichole never fully expressed how all of it felt for her. I know now that keeping those feelings inside may not have been healthy for her. We were doing our best, but there's always more to learn.

Today, Nichole refers to Tina as her bonus mom, and Mike as her bonus dad. That kind of blended family doesn't come from luck. It comes from years of choosing self-regulation, of leading with love, of placing the child's well-being above all else.

We stayed friends through it all. A friendship that feels like a quiet kind of love.

My wish for you in this reflection is that you and your family discover a new kind of unity, even if it's different than before. Be patient; it takes time to rebuild and there is no single timeline. More than anything, I hope your commitment to your child's emotional well-being guides you forward.

xo,

Christina

JOURNAL MOMENT 1: Telling the Children

When you feel ready, find a quiet space and take a few moments for yourself. You don't have to answer everything. Begin where it feels natural. Let these questions guide you toward what matters most right now, for you and your child. If it feels too soon, that's okay too. Simply come back when you're ready. This space is yours. You may have thought of some of your own ideas during this reflection. When you're ready, make an entry in your journal.

How will you care for yourself during this process?

If you have already told your children, take some time to journal. You can use the questions below to reflect.

Will you tell the children together? If not, what challenges will prevent this? Are they issues that can be worked through? Do you have a plan to deliver a consistent message? Do you and your former partner need to meet first and discuss the details?

Where and when will you have this conversation? Can you choose a time and place that allows for calm and preparation?

How will you calm and control your emotions first?

Do you need anyone else there for support?

How will you keep the conversation free from adult emotions?

Will your children feel safe and loved?

Are you prepared for their reactions?

What support might they need from you? Are you prepared to provide that support?

Are your plans truly in the best interest of the children?

Will you need professional guidance to navigate this process?

What other ideas do you have from this reflection that you could journal?

From left to right: Me and Tina being goofy at a local animal rescue zoo 2019

Reflection Two:
Finding Your Therapy

PROMPT 2

Take a quiet moment. What does healing look like for you? Not just survival, but true healing. If not therapy, then what? There is a therapeutic method out there for everyone. You just need to find what helps you. What are the tools, people, practices, or spaces that help you feel more whole, more grounded, more connected to yourself? What stress is your body carrying right now, and what is your body asking you to release? Take a moment to find some space to release what is not currently serving you. Find your therapy. Work to read through this reflection and process it without self-judgment.

I DIDN'T EXPECT therapy to help me at all. At first, it felt like one more thing I didn't have time or energy for. Something in me knew I had to try. Finding a therapist took time I didn't feel I had. It was harder than I imagined. I met with five different people before I made a connection. I was searching for more than someone to talk to. I also needed a spiritual connection, someone who aligned with my beliefs and values.

I remember sitting with the first woman. She was nice, but she immediately jumped into telling me about herself, running through her resume like she was trying to prove something to me. It didn't feel right. The second woman I met with asked me at the end of the session if I felt I needed medication. I didn't know what to say. *Did I really seem that bad?* I left feeling unsure, even more overwhelmed. The third one talked about God too much in the first session. I wasn't looking for someone to judge me based on my beliefs. She made me feel like there was only one way and that I was going to be judged if I didn't align.

As a counselor now, it seems funny to me that those early sessions contained lots of what-not-to-do moments. It just kept going, and I thought, *Am I ever going to find a therapist?* This was another example of me sticking to something I knew was right. At times, I wanted to give up and forget therapy. It was too hard, but then I found Evelyn and worked with her for three years. She helped me heal.

During my first session with her, she listened intently, providing me with the space I needed; she built rapport and trust. She was exactly what I'd been searching for. Therapists are not easy to find, but I found someone who connected with my energy and helped me work through the heaviness I carried. In Evelyn's presence, I believed that

I was a great mom and a great person, even when I couldn't feel it.

She started the pathway to my healing, and I started to do a lot of work on myself. A few sessions in, we spoke about my inability to let go of all the hurt I had caused. It was then that she said to me, "Remember, Christina, that every marriage, every divorce, every relationship does not involve one single person." She helped me see that what happened to me, to us, was not my fault, and it wasn't anyone else's fault. It was not about blaming.

There were times in my sessions when I felt ashamed to go too deep. Talking with a stranger about my deepest issues and secrets felt unsafe at first, but Evelyn continued to support me. She gained my trust through zero judgment, never responding unfavorably when I shared, validating my concerns, and helping me dig deeper. One day during our session, the deep conversation of my early relationship with Scott morphed into a deep dive into my childhood and my parents' relationship. Healing asks more of us than we expect.

I realized I couldn't be afraid to dig beneath that old belief that life was supposed to look perfect, even when it wasn't. *Who would think that going to therapy for my divorce would drum up my childhood?* Well, it did, and that was huge for me. The biggest thing stemming from that time in my life was not only my divorce, but some guilt I'd held onto from way back when I was a teen. You see, one of my biggest issues with guilt was not being able to protect my little brother from being bullied. I had no idea how deep this was until my therapist took me through it all. The healing kept going—healing I didn't even know I needed. *That was the turning point. The path that set me free.* Therapy is hard work, lots of tears and deep-seated pain, but work that heals.

Funny how energy goes out into the universe and returns to you. After digging deep into the pains of my childhood, I learned that my brother was also doing healing work. Well, he called me one day. He told me that the bullying he experienced was never my fault. How did he know I needed to hear that? How did he know that the timing of that conversation, after all these years, was perfect? I cried, and we cried together. I thanked him for his call. It couldn't have come at a more powerful time. For both of us, healing had begun. I believe in the power of the universe now more than ever.

Looking back, I also wish we had done family therapy together. Scott and I each had our therapists, but I wish we also had a family therapist and maybe even a therapist for Nichole. We were on the cusp of a generational overlap between therapy being considered a weakness and a now very accepted practice. Therapy helped me heal. Remember, healing isn't one path; it's a series of choices we keep making. So, when my therapy ended, I kept going in a different way. Today, I am no longer in therapy with a professional psychologist. My therapy is more spiritual, combined with wellness-based practices.

I remember feeling empathy toward my friend Lisa, who was going through a divorce. Her kids were young and suffering so badly from the brutal nature of their parents' divorce. She had finally found a therapist who dealt with younger children such as hers. This therapist later encouraged her and her former partner to join in on sessions to support the children. She then started meeting with them privately to discuss some changes they should make that could be crucial to the children moving forward. During this time, both she and her ex didn't appreciate that this therapist was encouraging them to stop fighting, stop blaming, and stop the violence the children were caught up in. I was so happy to hear about this counseling, because the kids needed advocacy. Unfortunately, they stopped seeing her, and so did the children because they didn't like that she was telling them what to do. They were offended, so they stopped therapy altogether. I remember thinking to myself, *I really wish these two could just stop hating so much, because their children are suffering so badly.*

They never went back, and to this day, their kids are in the middle of their parents' battles. All these years later, they are adults themselves and still suffer through the constant mediation they have to navigate. They are now in therapy of their own, on the road to healing. One of them told me once, "My parents could learn something from all of the support you are providing Nichole during your most difficult changes." We have received comments like this often, making me want to tell our story.

MY STORY: CARRYING YEARS OF STRESS

Allow me to share a special story, one that reminds me of why my connection to spirit, as well as my mind, body, and soul connections, are so important to my current well-being.

In the summer of 2022, I met with a Gastroenterology surgeon in Boston. After carrying years of stress in my gut, it was time to remove nine inches of my compromised colon and begin healing from the diverticulitis that had caused me so much pain for seven-plus years. That summer, I took a three-month medical leave from my job. I had never taken medical leave in my entire life, but for this surgery, I had no choice. I would consider this time off somewhat of a sabbatical. I did a ton of self-reflection on the things in my life that contributed to my stress. Like most of us, my job was not helping. I made a list of pros and cons in my role as an Administrator. Fortunately, the good outweighed the bad, but that wasn't solving the stress issues.

I decided to go see a Hypnotist. She was amazing! During my session, the message Spirit sent through her (for me) was one of the most powerful messages I might ever receive. The message was, *My power is in the things I can control, and I will let Spirit take the things out of my control.* I mean, *this is something we could all live by, right?* Now it was time to start my self-journey toward diving into this message. What did that mean for my daily life? That summer, I made so many changes in my life. It was my truest therapy of all.

My spiritual journey didn't start with certainty. It started in pain. I was raised Catholic and followed all the sacraments growing up, but after graduating high school, I slowly drifted from that path. We married in a Catholic church because my parents mean so much to me. For years, I didn't feel much connection to Spirit. Life was full: raising our daughter, working long hours, trying to build a home. Self-care was something I didn't yet understand.

It wasn't until the divorce that I began to open to spirituality again. I was broken and lost, and I needed something beyond logic. At first, *I felt like I had failed, not just as a partner or parent, but as someone who had broken a sacred rule I'd been taught never to cross:* the sacrament of marriage, the sacred, until death-do-us-part commitment. My therapist helped me start to release that belief. I began to work on understanding myself, not punishing myself. In that work, I found my connection to God again. I feel Spirit in my body now. I deepened that connection through meditation, through stillness, through listening.

That spiritual awareness didn't just help me feel less alone, it helped me find direction. Over time, my beliefs began guiding me toward a new life, showing me how to face fear and reminding me that I was never alone. I believe

God led me to this work. I believe it's how I wrote this book. It's how I continue to savor the moments I have. It's what gives me strength.

These days, my therapy is connection. I set two alarms in the morning: one fifteen minutes before I need to get up, and one for the real time. In those fifteen minutes, I meditate, express gratitude, or cuddle with my 91-pound dog Lucas. That tiny shift changes everything for me, as I used to roll over right when the alarm went off and check work emails. Of course, there was always something to read that started my day in stress mode. Someone once said, *Don't let the day start you; you start the day.* That always stuck with me, and it works. The day is much better when I kick it off my way.

Instead of rushing, I create space. I give thanks, I ask to be guided. I pause throughout the day, even if it's just for five minutes, lights off, doing breathwork in silence. I recharge, and on the drive home through the forest, I breathe more. I call my husband and shift into family mode. This is my rhythm now, but make no mistake, the rhythm breaks down regularly where stress exceeds calmness; it is human nature. It is a constant back and forth, trying to get back to peace. There are times when it feels impossible to maintain, weeks at a time where stress overtakes me. All we can do is keep focusing on what's within our power to influence. I stay away from trying to perfect any of it, and work to let my spirit take over the things that are out of my control.

One of my leaders once said to me, "Christina, nobody is telling you that you cannot take time for yourself before work; nobody is telling you that you can't leave early to attend a family event." The point is constant reflection on the things you can control. Are you bringing this stress on yourself, or is something else bringing it on? If it is you, how will you make changes? If it is something else, is it controllable? Can it be fixed? If not, can you just let it go and stop carrying it? After all, if it's beyond your reach, why let it drain your energy? Often, it is only we who are truly affected by it all. So, why not try and redirect the negative feelings into something more positive? Something that can make us feel happy instead of sad. I know this is easier said than done. Work toward change in small increments and retrain your mind; it works.

I just keep using the tools I have, allowing Spirit to guide me, focusing on what's good in my life, and letting gratitude take the wheel. I start calm, try to stay calm, and hope to end calm. It's not perfect, but I show up for it daily.

My wish for you is that you find what truly heals you and keep moving toward it, for the sake of you and your family.

xo,

Christina

JOURNAL MOMENT 2: Professional Guidance

Only when you feel ready, sit with your journal, find a quiet space, and take time with these questions. You don't have to answer them all. Just let them guide you toward what matters most right now, for you and your child. Take a moment to reflect: How will you get through this, with or without your partner? Some questions may not apply to your story, or maybe you've already faced them, but they can still help you reflect and write. When you're ready, make an entry in your journal.

How are you currently caring for yourself, emotionally, mentally and physically?

Have you thought about the possible need for therapy or other support systems?

If you have already found your therapy, take some time to journal about it. You can use the questions below to reflect.

What types of ideas calm you? A run, Yoga, gardening, a good movie?

Will you pursue some form of therapy, and if so, can your family do it with you sometime?

What types of therapy can you attend with your family that could support the children?

How might therapy benefit your children?

If therapy isn't the right path, what other support systems could help you navigate this process?

Are your plans truly in the best interest of the children?

Have you considered seeking professional guidance to ensure you have the right tools for healing?

What other ideas do you have from this reflection that you could journal?

Reflection Three: Stages of Grief

PROMPT 3

Take a moment to sit down with your loved ones and ask how they are currently feeling, from their perspective. Listen openly and without judgment, allowing them to express their feelings. After your conversation, reflect on what you learned and write down your thoughts, emotions, and any new insights in your journal. Consider how their viewpoints might shape your understanding of what is happening and how it can guide you now and to move forward.

DIVORCE IS A loss, and with loss comes grief. You and your children will go through the emotional stages commonly associated with grief: denial, anger, bargaining, depression, and acceptance. Understanding these stages can help you process your emotions and support your children through theirs.

As I've mentioned, we've seen many people close to

us walk the difficult road of divorce. We've seen how pain and fear can cloud everything, and how often children get caught in the crossfire. I don't believe anyone is intentionally mean or vicious, or that anyone in their right mind would intentionally hurt someone they love, especially their children. I know emotions can easily take over; I have personally lived it. They can cloud judgment and lead to pain, even trauma. In some cases, they can trigger mental health struggles that weren't there before.

There is more help available now than ever before, but recognizing the need and reaching for it is often the hardest step. If it goes unmanaged, the emotional environment can become unsafe for everyone.

Denial: *This can't be happening; this isn't going how I hoped.* I denied my breakdown and believed Scott felt the same. I was in denial that the divorce was going to happen.

Anger: *Why did this happen? Why can't I fix this?* Frustration, hurt, and the pain of things not being easier. I had always been the one who held things together. So why couldn't I hold this?

Bargaining: *If only I had done this differently.* Trying to find ways to undo or change the past. Many times, I thought about going back to my marriage *just to stop all the pain.* Realizing that going back would be for all the wrong reasons was anything but simple. It would've been easier to go back and pretend nothing had broken.

Depression: *The weight of reality sinking in.* Feeling

lost, exhausted, and hopeless. Months of feeling antisocial, choosing days on the couch without showering over a healthy time out with family and friends.

Acceptance: *This is my life now.* Finding peace, letting go, and moving forward. Lots of healing work and self-care.

MY STORY: HOW I COPED WITH GRIEF

In the early days, I was barely functioning. I lived on cigarettes, coffee, and wine—whatever it took to get through the day. I couldn't eat without throwing up. I couldn't get out of bed without dragging myself. I was painfully thin. I felt like I had ruined everything. The guilt of breaking up my family consumed me. I kept wondering if I should go back to Scott.

I wanted so badly to protect Nichole. I was so focused on managing my own pain and guilt that I didn't realize how much she needed me to let her in.

Looking back, I think she wasn't doing as well as I believed at the time. She was talking to her friends, which I told myself was good, but friends aren't therapists. We needed professional guidance. I was guessing my way through it, and I still carry guilt about that. I sheltered her too much. I may have kept her from crying, from processing, from sitting in the pain with me in a healthy way. I thought I was protecting her, but I may have robbed her of something important. Figuring out what's healthy and what's harmful isn't always obvious. Sometimes, it takes guidance. I was so afraid I would overshare. In hindsight, I wasn't allowing any sharing at all.

I should have shared more with her—not about everything, not about affairs or adult pain, but enough to help her feel seen. Enough to help her grieve alongside me. I think we both needed that. If I could go back, I'd get us into family therapy from the start. I'd ask for help. I wouldn't try to hold it all alone.

As time evolved, I found support from my mom, my best friend, my therapist, and Spirit. However, even with that, it was hard. Acceptance didn't come all at once. It came in waves. It still does. It's not linear. It's something we grow into over time, with support. Everyone's version of acceptance looks different.

The stages of grief aren't a checklist. They rise and fall. They blend and return. With the right support, they soften. The edges get less sharp. Even when acceptance slips away, it can return. What matters is that you keep reaching for it.

If you're spiraling, please get help. It doesn't have to be just you. Support might be a therapist, a trusted friend, a group, or just one honest talk with someone who's been there. Sometimes, just knowing you're not the only one feeling this way is enough to take the next step.

I judged myself constantly, and others judged me too. People didn't ask how I was; they just said, "You had everything; what did you do?" They had no idea what I was holding inside. There were days I was so low I could have driven off a bridge. That's how dark it got. Through all of that turmoil, I wish I had found a way to share a healthy emotional space with Nichole. I wish we had grieved together, even just a little. Finding the balance between healthy sharing and overprotecting your children is not easy. There is a balance, and it can be very healthy for everyone to engage.

Doing this alone is heavy, and when you're stuck in grief and guilt, it's easy to lose perspective. You may think you're protecting your child, but even unintentional damage can leave a mark.

I used to wear oversized clothes to hide my body. I wanted to vanish. I wish someone had told me earlier that therapy wasn't a weakness. Back then, it still carried a quiet stigma. In our family, therapy and divorce just weren't something we talked about. Fortunately, that's changed now. People talk about it openly, and it's more accepted.

If I could leave you with one thing, it's this: Wanting to protect your children is natural. Part of that protection means going on the journey with them, not around them. You're not meant to carry this alone.

DENIAL

I imagine all of us held on to a level of false hope for a long time, believing we might get back together. It's something we don't always say out loud, but it's there. That small voice that kept saying, *Maybe this isn't the end. Maybe if we wait it out, maybe if we say the right thing, it'll turn around.*

Sometimes, people simply grow apart. Even if there's still love somewhere in the background, even if there are moments that still feel like family. That's a hard truth. As parents, we don't just face it alone; we face it while trying to hold our children steady. They're watching. They're feeling it. They need us to tell them, "You're safe, and everything is going to be okay."

Selfish or selfless? That question haunted me. Was I projecting my own denial onto Nichole, or was I helping her process hers? Was I protecting her, or was I shielding myself?

That's what it becomes. Anger. Resentment. That leftover hope tangled up with bitterness. I've seen what happens when you are in denial of the truths you are facing. When you say things that you don't mean, but your kids hear them anyway.

Kids absorb everything. Your silence. Your words. Your body language. If you're not careful, they start to believe they're the problem. They stop feeling safe.

When I felt myself spiraling, I had to learn how to bring myself back. I started with my breath. Deep, slow breaths from the belly, not the chest. I used calming words: *Shhh, relax, I've got this, calm down.* I'd repeat them to myself until my body started to listen. Sometimes I'd go to a peaceful memory in my mind, something soft, something safe. I would imagine something I wanted to feel. I would practice this just long enough to take the edge off.

Therapy gave me tools. One of the most powerful was

something called cognitive restructuring. It means learning how to redirect thoughts and teach your mind new learning. *This sucks* became *This is hard, but I can handle it. Everything is terrible* turned into *This is hard, but it's normal. I can't do this* shifted to *This won't be easy, but I can take it one step at a time. It's not forever. I don't have to stay in this place.* You learn to pause your thoughts and guide them toward something steadier. To reroute them, to change the way your brain is processing the emotion. It's not pretending, it's survival.

I had to stop using words like always and never. *We will never get through this*, or *This always happens*. That kind of language locks you in. It convinces you that nothing can change, but things can change if you let them.

Denial doesn't show up all at once. It's not a single moment. It's a process. It comes, and it leaves, and it comes back again. This process is healthy; it's okay. Every stage of grief matters. There's no timeline, no straight path. You find what works, and you hold onto it.

For me, support mattered. I didn't get through this alone. I had my mom, my best friend, my therapist, Spirit. That was my team. That's what helped me keep going. That's what helped me to keep showing up for Nichole when I felt like I had nothing left.

Remember, your children are watching. How you move through these stages shapes how they will move through them too.

JOURNAL MOMENT 3A: Denial

Only when you feel ready, sit with your journal, find a quiet space, and take time with these questions. You don't have to answer them all. Just let them guide you toward what matters most right now, for you and your child. Take a moment to reflect: How will you get through this, with or without your partner? They may not all be relevant to your story (or maybe you've already been through these), but they will help you write it. When you're ready, make an entry in your journal.

State one or more ways you are currently caring for yourself.

Now consider the stage of denial in your personal story.

How are you feeling in this moment?

What thoughts or beliefs are you holding that may reflect denial?

How do you think your former partner is feeling?

Are you both offering a united message to your children?

What could you be doing differently?

Are your plans truly in the best interest of your child?

Will you need professional guidance through this process? You'll find examples and resources in the wellness section of Reflection 9 to help make the process feel more accessible.

What other ideas do you have from this reflection that you could journal?

ANGER

When I realized I was going to leave my marriage, there were times that I was mad, downright angry. What did I do to deserve all of this? I am a good person. Why? I was angry at Scott for not acknowledging our problems sooner. I was angry with friends for judging me so hard. I was angry with family because they were taking sides and shutting me out. I was even angry with God at some point, because I had always felt supported in my life, like I was on the path of greatness, and now it was all falling apart. I was angry with myself for not being able to fix it all, for being unable to keep the family unit together.

I think about my anger a lot. Imagine if Nichole had ever heard me say, "I hate you." Even if it wasn't meant for her. Even if I said it to Scott in a moment of rage. A sentence like that stays with a child forever. I remember when I was at my lowest, thinking my life had been a complete waste. In the next thought, I would remember how lucky I was to have such a beautiful daughter, family, and friends. Imagine if I had ever said something like that to Nichole? "My whole life has been a complete waste." I feel certain she would think, *Thanks, Mom, I am a complete waste!* Your words, while not always intentional, can be taken literally, and some things can't be unsaid.

Turning a child against the other parent, consciously or not, is another form of damage. I know people who've done it. I've felt the pull of it in moments of pain. If you're drowning in resentment, seek help. Try to catch yourself. Everything is in your delivery.

Anger is normal. However, if you don't manage it, it doesn't just hurt your ex, it hurts you. Most of all, it hurts children. I didn't show anger about our situation, because the truth was that no matter how much it hurt, it was our new norm.

Anger is a primary emotion, meaning it is an underlying feeling resulting from an experience. It is real and an emotion that needs to be dealt with to move forward and heal. Anger is healthy when managed. It is normal, and once you understand this, it is easier to process.

Holding onto anger can be detrimental to your health, however. It impacts your physical and mental wellbeing. Be careful, because anger can turn into grudges and create ongoing stress. While anger is natural and a normal part of the healing process, it is important to let go of it to foster a healthier emotional state of mind.

Here are eight things I learned that helped me deal with the anger when it came:

1. Stop and consider why you're angry.
2. Look for what you can change in the moment.
3. Notice your emotional triggers.
4. Set new boundaries where you need them.
5. Use your anger to motivate something constructive.
6. Let go of what doesn't matter.
7. Move your body: walk, stretch, breathe.
8. Channel the anger into something that helps, not harms.

JOURNAL MOMENT 3B: Anger

Only when you feel ready, sit with your journal and center your-self to start thinking and writing about the anger you feel today.

State one or more ways you are currently caring for yourself.

Now consider the stage of anger in your personal story.

How are you feeling in this moment?

What thoughts or beliefs are you holding that may reflect anger?

How do you think your former partner is feeling?

Are you both offering a united message to your children?

What could you be doing differently?

Are your plans truly in the best interest of your children?

Will you need professional guidance through this process? You'll find examples and resources in the wellness section of Reflection 9 to help make the process feel more accessible.

What other ideas do you have from this reflection that you could journal?

BARGAINING

I look back and think maybe therapy could have helped fix things in our marriage. Maybe we would've stood a chance. The truth is, we had been trying to fix it for years. I felt sad and guilty, like I had failed. I kept wondering if I had given up too soon.

At the time, I wasn't as spiritual. I didn't have much to lean on except my own willpower, and that wasn't always enough. Now, I turn to Spirit first. Back then, I thought staying strong meant hiding what I felt. I was trying to hold it together, thinking that if I looked okay on the outside, everything would be fine. Unfortunately, it wasn't. I needed to let it all out. I deserved to be cared for too, and I didn't know how to give that to myself enough.

There were so many moments when I thought maybe Scott and I would get back together, just to stop the pain. That's what bargaining looks like. It's when your mind reaches for any version of the story that hurts the least, and it's natural. Adults do it and children probably do it even more.

Children will sometimes try to bring their parents closer again by asking for shared time, giving gifts, or saying things they hope might soften the split. It's not manipulation, it's grief. That's why we have to be consistent. We have to be honest without being harsh.

I remember trying to explain things to Nichole in a way that wouldn't hurt her. I said, "We're not really like husband

and wife anymore, we're more like brother and sister. We'll always be friends, and we'll always be here for you." Funny how I felt that the word "always" here was a safe bet. I didn't want her holding on to false hope. I wanted her to feel secure, even in the middle of change.

Have you ever seen the movie *The Parent Trap*? It's a great example of how kids think, what they might wish for. The two twin girls scheming, plotting to try and get their parents back together. It is not a false hope for kids; it is very real and probably takes years to go away, or maybe the hope never goes away.

If you're in this stage, be mindful of your words. Don't talk about court or lawyers in front of your kids. Don't make promises you can't keep. Don't let your fear or your guilt confuse them. Bargaining can make you feel desperate, but your children need clarity as much as they need comfort.

If you're overwhelmed, ask for help. *You don't have to figure this out alone. Therapy isn't only for crisis, it's for guidance.* It's a place to be honest, to get support, and to find a path forward for you and your children.

JOURNAL MOMENT 3C: Bargaining

Only when you feel ready, sit with your journal, find a quiet space, and take time with these questions. You don't have to answer them all. Just let them guide you toward what matters most right now, for you and your child. Take a moment to reflect: How will you get through this, with or without your partner? They may not all be relevant to your story, or maybe you've already been through these, but they will help you write it. When you're ready, make an entry in your journal.

State one or more ways you are currently caring for yourself.

Consider the stage of bargaining.

Are the messages you're delivering to your children consistent?

Are you communicating clearly?

Are you reaching for a version of the story that hurts the least, even if it's not the healthiest one?

Is your child reaching, hoping, or asking questions?

How will you respond with honesty and care?

What can you do to stay mindful of your own well-being while supporting them?

Are your plans truly in the best interest of your children?

Will you need professional guidance through this process?

If you're feeling overwhelmed, what specific self-care practices or tools can help?

What other ideas do you have from this reflection that you could journal?

DEPRESSION

Divorce meant facing the truth: life would never go back to how it was. I was living alone for the first time in my entire life. Every task felt new, and every responsibility felt heavier. I was scared, overwhelmed, and completely drained. I slept on the couch; I wasn't eating. I couldn't sleep through the night. I cried over small things like commercials, empty rooms, a dish left in the sink. There was a constant ache in my chest. Anxiety would grip me out of nowhere. I wasn't functioning. That's when I realized I might be having a breakdown, and I needed help.

As I mentioned, finally connecting with the right therapist supported a shift forward. I gave up a few comforts to afford those sessions because my insurance didn't cover the one therapist I finally connected with. I made it work because I needed help and I couldn't keep going like I was. The help is out there; you just have to reach for it.

Looking back, I wish I had been more open. I kept everything inside. I isolated myself because I wanted people to think I was fine. After all, I was always known as the strong one, the organized one, the person who had an answer for everything.

My depression was embarrassing to me back then. I didn't want anyone to see me as weak. Depression is a natural response when you are experiencing something as serious as divorce. Showing your vulnerable side to others is healthy and helps you move forward. When we shield our children too much, we risk teaching them to hide their feelings. We end up teaching them that sadness is unsafe, or that it's ours to carry for them. They have feelings they need to express, too. They need space to process. Therapy can help with that. It can help you find a way to talk about hard things without handing them your weighted burdens.

Years after starting therapy, I slowly began to rebuild. I got deeper into self-care. I began paying attention to what

I ate, how I moved, and how I spoke to myself. I even went back to school and studied nutrition—the first time in years I'd chosen something for myself. Therapy didn't fix everything right away, but it helped me take one small step, and then another. Eventually, those steps became a life I wanted to keep showing up for.

JOURNAL MOMENT 3D: Depression

Only when you feel ready, sit with your journal, find a quiet space, and take time with these questions. You don't have to answer them all. Just let them guide you toward what matters most right now, for you and your child. Take a moment to reflect: How will you get through this, with or without your partner? They may not all be relevant to your story, or maybe you've already been through these, but they will help you write it. When you're ready, make an entry in your journal.

State one or more ways you are currently caring for yourself.

Consider the stage of depression. Are you facing it?

Are you seeking guidance to help you through? If so, what guidance is working?

Is your former partner struggling too?

Is your child showing signs of sadness or withdrawal?

How are you managing and coping with these realities?

Are your plans truly in the best interest of your child?

Will you need professional guidance during this time?

Professional assistance might be more important than ever now; depression is very serious.

What other ideas do you have from this reflection that you could journal?

ACCEPTANCE

It took me four years to fully accept that we were never going back to what we once were. The guilt softened, the pain eased, but it never disappeared completely, and maybe it never will. The five stages of grief aren't linear.

They loop; they pause. For me, it was more like a constant tornado that took three or four years to work through.

Acceptance didn't mean the sadness disappeared. It meant I stopped resisting what was real. I let go of the life I thought I was meant to have and started learning how to live inside the one I had.

My therapist helped me get there. She never rushed me. She validated everything I felt, over and over. She kept reminding me that my whole world was being rebuilt. I'd spent over twenty years building a marriage, a family, a sense of security, and it was all changing. Finances, roles, identity. It felt like the ground had vanished beneath me. Therapy gave me something to hold on to. She reminded me that grief isn't the same as failure and that I wasn't crazy for still feeling pain.

I hadn't always been able to express my emotions. As I mentioned earlier, if anything, I was suppressing my emotions in the most severe manner. Therapy helped me see that processing emotion was something I could do safely.

I also learned to protect our space. Adult conversations happened behind closed doors, never where Nichole could hear. I had to ask myself, *Am I saying this to support her, or to take a dig at Scott?* That question kept me grounded. While Nichole was getting older and growing up, the reality of divorce was still fresh for many years.

Acceptance, for me, was about choosing to keep going. I had to take care of myself while still doing what was right for Nichole. That meant not falling apart in front of her. It meant holding the heavy tears until she wasn't there to see them. When I couldn't hold on, it meant reaching out. I called a friend, I booked a session, I let someone in.

Those earlier modes like denial, anger, bargaining, and depression stopped running the show. What helped me move through? Reassurance from people who really knew me: my therapist, my closest friends, and Spirit. Eventually, I received reassurance from myself. I needed that steady presence around me to keep walking forward when everything felt broken.

Acceptance didn't mean I was fine. It meant I believed I would be, *eventually*, and that was enough.

JOURNAL MOMENT 3E: Acceptance

Only when you feel ready, sit with your journal, find a quiet space, and take time with these questions. Not every question will apply. Use the ones that help you reflect on what matters most for you and your child. Take a moment to reflect: How will you get through this, with or without your partner? They may not all be relevant to your story, or maybe you've already been through these, but they will help you write it. When you're ready, make an entry in your journal.

State one or more ways you're currently caring for yourself.

Consider the stage of acceptance. Where are you in it?

Where is your family unit in this stage?

Are you allowing your children to experience their emotions?

How are you supporting those emotions?

Reflect on who you're leaning on for support, or what practices are helping you move forward.

Are your plans truly in the best interest of the children?

Will you need professional guidance to help you through?

What other ideas do you have from this reflection that you could journal?

COPING WITH GRIEF

Our divorce wasn't just something I went through; it was something we all had to process through. The family unit we once knew was changing, and that shift brought with it a sense of loss that each of us had to face in our own way.

Not every family or individual can or should process grief in the same way. Some might lean on faith. Others might turn to friends, therapy, or quiet time alone. What matters is that you don't ignore it. Suppressed emotions don't disappear; they find other ways to show up or to surface, sometimes in ways that cause more harm than good. I've seen it, and I've lived it.

There's no single answer. One question helped me again and again: *Is this helpful, or is this just unloading?* That was the question I asked myself before any hard conversation, especially with Nichole. If I was having a hard day, I'd reach out to a trusted friend, to my mom, or to Spirit. I had to channel the emotions somewhere safe.

In situations where there's been abuse or deep trauma, the grief becomes more complicated. You might need professional support to untangle what's safe, what's healthy, and what needs to be protected. The most important thing is staying honest with yourself and with your child. If you're not okay, say that. Take the steps to find support. You don't have to figure it all out alone.

I know this book won't be for every reader. Some stories here might feel too raw, too close, too far from your own. My hope is that by sharing mine, you feel less alone in yours. That somewhere in these pages, you find permission to feel it all—messy, imperfect, real—and continue to move forward, healthy and happy.

My wish for you and your family is that you move through the stages of grief with as much unity and care as possible, always with your child's well-being at heart.

xo,

Christina

JOURNAL MOMENT 3F: Coping with Grief

Only when you feel ready, sit with your journal, find a quiet space, and take time with these questions. You don't have to answer them all. Just let them guide you toward what matters most right now, for you and your child. Take a moment to reflect: How will you get through this, with or without your partner? They may not all be relevant to your story, or maybe you've already been through these. Either way, they will help you write it. When you're ready, make an entry in your journal.

How can you move through the stages of grief in a healthy way, for you and your children?

Can you and your former partner unite through this process?

List three ideas you can practice moving forward to support your health.

What actions and approaches will help you process your emotions?

Create a list of what is working and what is not working so you can clearly see where to continue your focus.

How would you describe your relationship with your children now?

How will you dive deeper into your children's feelings? What are they experiencing?

What is your former partner experiencing?

List some examples of challenges you are facing.

How can you work together to start resolving them?

How are you processing your feelings?

Are you being mindful of the words you express?

What feelings do you need to share with your children right now?

What does a true, healthy conversation look like?

Do you or your children need therapy?

How can you help your children pull through the stages of change?

Can you be more vulnerable for your children in a healthy manner?

Remember, this is a lot. Take your time, and keep coming back to this reflection over and over again. Journal now, journal later, keep journaling. The process is evolving. You are amazing!

What other ideas do you have from this reflection that you could journal?

Reflection Four:
Reaching Out to
Other Parties

PROMPT 4

Before beginning this reflection, take a moment to ground yourself in the connections that matter. Only when you feel ready, find a quiet space, sit with your journal, and reflect on the key people who support you and your children. You might sit with a trusted friend, go for a walk, or simply close your eyes and think about those who have been there for you. Who offers stability, guidance, or a listening ear? Use this reflection to consider the relationships that support you.

DIVORCE DOESN'T HAPPEN in isolation. Its impact reaches beyond the couple, touching families, friendships, schools, and communities. Connecting with key people such as extended family, teachers, and caregivers can make a meaningful difference. This reflection focuses on how to communicate thoughtfully with those in your child's world, so they can help provide the stability and support your child needs during this transition.

Teachers, coaches, and school counselors can work to support children in circumstances of divorce. They can assist with lunch money, resources, help children navigate through custody battles, ensuring information reaches both homes, especially if parents aren't communicating well. Maybe they are just simply watching for any changes that seem a bit off for your child. Whatever the reality, there are people who should know, so they can support and assist.

Nichole was thriving in many ways during this time. A straight-A student, a member of the National Honor Society, an All-Star Cheerleader, a Black Belt in Karate. She poured herself into academics and sports with a kind of focus that felt like resilience. Scott and I knew she was doing well on the surface, but we also knew the toll a divorce could take beneath it. So, we took a proactive approach. We reached out directly to the people who saw her most: her teachers, coaches, and the parents of her closest friends. Whether in person or by phone, we explained what was happening at home. We told them we were going through a divorce, but that we intended to do what was best for Nichole.

We asked them to keep an eye out for anything that seemed off: signs of emotional withdrawal, sudden shifts in behavior, anything that might suggest she was struggling under the weight of it all. Most of these adults had known Nichole for years. They understood who she was at her baseline. That gave us some peace. We trusted that if something changed, they would notice, and they would tell us.

Her cheerleading coach spent more time with her than almost anyone outside our home. He was warm, receptive, and took our concerns seriously. Her guidance counselor at school also stepped in, checking in regularly and collaborating with her teachers to ensure nothing slipped through the cracks. It felt like people cared, not just about her as a student or athlete, but as a whole person. That meant everything to both of us.

I didn't face resistance when I reached out, but that didn't make it easy. Each time I had to explain, I felt a wave of shame—the shame of getting divorced. It was a quiet feeling of failure. Saying it out loud meant accepting it again and again, and sharing that part of our lives was painful. Whenever I opened up, I was met with understanding. In hindsight, I think people respected that we were being so intentional in protecting Nichole's emotional well-being. It helped dissolve the shame a little. I got the feeling they didn't get many inquiries like ours from other families experiencing divorce.

Scott and I weren't perfectly aligned in every detail, but we were aligned in what mattered. I handled most of the logistics, like calling teachers, writing emails, and keeping everyone informed, and he supported me fully. He showed up, emotionally and practically, whenever it counted. That sense of unity didn't come easily; we had moments that felt unbearable. The emotional wreckage of divorce, especially early on, can cloud even the simplest conversations. Nevertheless, we pushed through it for our daughter. We kept coming back to one truth: she came first. Even if we didn't feel like partners anymore, we still had to parent like a team.

We also encouraged Nichole to lean on others outside of us. She was close to Scott's sister, and my mom had always been someone she could turn to. I gently reminded her that if she ever needed to talk, and didn't feel ready to come to us, those women would always be there. I never needed to know what she said; that wasn't the point. I wanted her to have space, that's all. To this day, I imagine she shared things with others that I'll never hear about. In any case, I'm so glad she did. If that's what helped her get through the hardest parts, then I'm grateful for every one of those conversations I wasn't part of.

She had some close friends she could turn to, although that was always the scariest part. It was not knowing what she was doing out there, each time she left the house. I remember in the later years, she and I were packing up one of her apartments, and I inadvertently noticed some photos of a party she'd been at. I am sure my sweet little girl had some moments of craziness that I am happy I don't know the details about. I'm just thankful we made it through. Some things are better left in the past.

Looking back, I can imagine how she might have coped.

She kept busy, and that probably helped. She filled her days with school, cheerleading, karate, softball, and college applications. Movement gave her momentum. She didn't stall out; she stayed focused. It's not that she didn't feel the pain. We all did. Luckily, she had support from every direction. That web of care was woven from school, home, friends, and family. To this day, I hope it held her steady.

If you're reading this and wondering who to reach out to, start with the obvious: school, coaches, extended family, the parents of your child's closest friends. Let them know what's going on and ask them to keep an eye out. You don't need a big conversation, just an honest one. You're not asking them to fix anything; you're simply giving them the chance to notice, to care, to be there in ways you might not be able to.

You don't have to do this alone, and your child shouldn't have to either.

Outwardly, I was organized and proactive. Inside, I was unravelling.

Nichole poured herself into her routines, and I took comfort in that. Looking back, I will always feel like I should have done more. I should have helped her process what was happening, and not just moved through it. I think all loving parents feel like they can do more, no matter what the situation. We got through it all and our daughter is a very loving, caring, successful woman today. My point is that if you try your best and truly give it your all with the best intentions, hopefully it will all work itself out.

Scott and I stayed united when it came to parenting. No matter what was going on between us personally, we always checked in with each other before talking to teachers or coaches. We went to meetings together, making it clear our daughter came first. If something shifted in her, we wanted to know. I wonder what it felt like for Nichole to be surrounded by adults quietly monitoring her.

I remember sitting in the stands one summer at a softball game. It was one of the first events we attended after separating. Sitting in the stands at a softball game usually meant being in the same spot with all the same people. This night wasn't any different, except now, rather than walking into the stands together, we walked in apart, and it seemed like everyone knew it. Honestly, I think I was more paranoid about these things than they were true. It is normal to feel like everyone is judging, because in some cases, this is the truth. We sat down, Scott on one end of the bench and me on the other. There were lots of families in between us, and we knew most of them. I kept peeking down the bench, wondering how he was doing. One of the parents came up into the stands and deliberately sat next to me. I thought, *Great, here we go with the questions*, and felt shame.

To my surprise, this was different. The woman turned to me and said, "We are divorcing too. Please tell Nichole so she and Sara can support each other." I was so sad to hear it was happening to someone else. You feel so isolated sometimes that you forget there are other people going through the same things. In that moment, I felt a small sense of normalcy again. I honestly don't know if Nichole and Sara ever talked about their feelings, but I can only hope they both found peace along the way, in as many ways as possible.

Divorce shakes everything. When you reach out to the right people, it helps keep your child grounded. Even if you're falling apart inside, your child doesn't have to fall with you. There can still be solid ground beneath them; you just need to help build it.

My wish for you and your loved ones is that the connections you strengthen, whether with teachers, friends, or family, help you create a supportive foundation for your child's well-being.

xo,

Christina

JOURNAL MOMENT 4: Reaching Out

Only when you feel ready, sit with your journal, find a quiet space, and take time with these questions. You don't have to answer them all. Just let them guide you toward what matters most right now, for you and your child. Take a moment to reflect: How will you get through this with or without your partner? They may not all be relevant to your story, or maybe you've already been through these, but they will help you write it. Make an entry in your journal when you feel ready.

Maybe you have already notified some resources on this topic. Journal your experiences and use the questions below to reflect.

Consider who in your child's life needs to be informed about the changes they are going through. Maybe coaches, school counselors, therapists, family members, or parents of friends. What will you say to each of them?

Think about those who spend time with your child when you're not there. How can they help provide stability?

How will you cope with the changes your child might be facing?

You can build a strong support system, ensuring your child feels secure and understood even as life shifts around them. What information can you share?

Are there specific struggles you are noticing about your child that you can share with others to watch over?

Will you and your partner make these notifications together? If not, can you discuss how to possibly unite on this? If one of the resources needs to discuss your child, who should they call?

If it's one of you, will you be able to let the other know?

Do both parents need to know so they can navigate this together?

What tools can you offer here so your child can move through this ?

Are you meeting them where they are with a united message?

How can you avoid getting wrapped in your own feelings?

Are your plans truly in their best interest?

Will you need professional guidance to navigate this process?

What other ideas do you have from this reflection that you could journal?

Reflection Five: Navigating Separation & Custody

PROMPT 5

Find a quiet space where you can reflect without distractions. Take a deep breath and center yourself. This exercise will help you navigate the emotional and logistical shifts that come with separation and custody. Visualize a day in your child's life in this new reality. Picture their morning, their school day, their evenings. What changes do they experience? What remains the same? Now, shift perspectives. Imagine yourself as your child. What do they feel? What do you think they might need? After this visualization, write down any insights that come up. Are there small adjustments you can make to create more stability? Are there ways to communicate with your co-parent to ease transitions? Let this exercise guide you in making choices that support your child's well-being through this change.

SEPARATION DOESN'T JUST divide a household; it

disrupts everything: your routines, your finances, your sense of stability. The ground shifts under your feet, and just when you need clarity most, everything feels uncertain. For parents, the biggest challenge becomes staying grounded enough to create a sense of safety for your child, even while you're still finding your own footing.

Custody isn't just a legal arrangement; it's the daily reality of how your child moves between two homes, how they wake up, who helps with homework, who tucks them in. It's not about splitting time equally; it's about building something functional, something loving, something that reflects who your child is and what they need most right now. In most cases, they need both of you to survive all of this.

This part of the journey asks a lot. It requires honesty, compromise, and a willingness to focus on your child's experience above your own emotions. It's not easy, but it's possible to do this with care. It's okay to figure it out one conversation, one adjustment, one agreement at a time.

MY STORY: HOW I MOVED OUT

When I made the decision to move out, I was absolutely petrified. I had never lived alone before, not once in my entire life. I grew up in my parents' house, then moved into an apartment with Scott, and from there, we continued building a life together in different homes over the years. This new road was something else entirely. At thirty-eight years old, for the first time, I was stepping into a home that would be mine and mine alone.

The thought of it terrified me, and the nights felt endless. I couldn't bring myself to sleep in the upstairs bedroom, so I stayed on the couch downstairs for over a year. I told myself it was temporary, but the fear didn't go away. It wasn't just about the silence; it was the weight of everything that had happened, all pressing down at once. I was unravelling emotionally. This move, although necessary, felt like one more piece I didn't know how to carry.

Still, I chose to leave our beautiful home. It would have been easier in some ways to stay and ask Scott to leave, but I knew deep down that doing so would have added even more pain. We were already in such a fragile place,

From left to right: Scott, Tina, our son-in-law, our daughter, Mike, me, my mom & dad at a winery for our daughter's birthday 2013

and staying would have made it worse. I didn't want to create more hurt than we were already facing.

We had to prepare for another hard conversation with our daughter. Scott and I sat down together to figure out how we would tell her. I had already started looking for another home by then. I wanted her to feel that, even with so much change, something solid would remain beneath her. That we weren't just breaking things apart, but were trying to build something new, something steady. It was one of the scariest moments of my life, and she must have been scared, too.

This change was one of the hardest for all of us, as it made everything real. There was no going back. I kept reminding myself that this wasn't our daughter's burden, it was ours. We told her not to worry. We told her that no matter what, we were still her parents. We wanted her to know that this didn't change how much we loved her, or how we would show up for her.

Later, when it came time to go to court, we hired ONE attorney to help us work through the logistics. We made a conscious decision not to involve child support or formal visitation orders. We wanted to manage things on our own, in a way that worked for Nichole. We trusted each other enough to do that. For some families, legal orders are necessary to ensure fairness, to protect children from conflict or harm. I believe that they should never be used to control a child; that's not what parenting is. The goal should always be to reduce harm, not add to it.

In situations where there's abuse, manipulation, or ongoing conflict, professional support becomes essential. You don't have to go through that alone. For us, even through the worst of times, we found a way to build something respectful. We chose what we hoped would be the least painful path. This intention was not just for us, but for her too. In this sense, we were luckier than most, and this was certainly a non-traditional method. In fact, I am pretty sure the divorce attorney we hired was in shock. She encouraged us not to take the road we planned to take. I am sure she had seen just about every problem that could arise, and that she was used to fights and not resolutions coming through her door. I imagine she talked about us for years to come, expecting that we didn't survive our arrangement.

As for us, we just wanted to finish this painful process and work to begin moving forward. We started running through assets, and it was clear to me that the attorney was on my side more than Scott's, wanting me to crush him in this area. But we stayed true to our decisions, and in the end, this helped ease some of our pain.

Eat Pray Love is my favorite movie; I've probably seen it twenty times. Even now, it still makes me emotional because I resonate so deeply with it. I would like to share with you some moments from the film.

In the beginning, Liz is in her first marriage and prays to God, asking him to give her a sign, literally saying, *Just tell me what to do, and I'll do it*. I was there. Every day, I waited for some sort of sign to help me fix things so I wouldn't end up divorced.

There's a part where she says, *The only thing harder than leaving was staying*. That hit me so hard. At the same time, the idea of staying often felt worse. I was suffocating in a tornado of emotional indecision.

Then, in the movie, when she's at the ashram in India, there's a scene where she looks back at her first wedding. That moment stuck with me because Scott and I had a very small wedding. We never had the big, beautiful wedding most girls dream of. We were practical, and this was the right decision at the time. We put the money toward a house instead, and I don't regret that.

Then there's the part where she talks about wanting to run away for a year to Italy, to eat food and feel alive again. She says something like, *I don't even have a pulse anymore*. I knew that feeling well. I wanted to run far and never turn back. I wanted to go away forever, to be by myself, but I didn't have that luxury. Of course, we cannot run away because our children need us.

Moving into the new house felt like a failure in some ways. We had worked so hard to build our homes, laying every brick, painting every wall ourselves. The last house was custom, beautiful, and filled with years of effort. Leaving it behind broke something in me. I took as much of it as I could to the new house to try to make it feel familiar for Nichole. However, I never felt comfortable there. I stayed for fifteen years, and I only sold it once I married Mike. That house held so many painful memories. It was where I grieved everything. Selling it was another new beginning, a fresh start, a healthy push forward.

I was not coping or healing well at all. I was so worried about everyone else that I started to lose myself. The guilt ran so deep I didn't think I could come back from it. I felt worthless. I'd get home from work, change into sweats, and crawl into bed. I had no energy for anything. I stopped wanting to be around people; the thought filled me with anxiety. I hated putting on a smile as if nothing was wrong. I didn't want pity, but neither did I know how to ask for help.

Getting out of bed felt impossible some days. Depression, guilt, and fear weighed me down. I still had to work, still had to show up for life, and I did it, but it drained me. I've always been a genuine, open person, and faking my emotions every day took everything out of me.

In the beginning, my daughter was my coping mechanism. Being a good mother to her was the only thing that kept me going. That was my anchor. Over time, I began to learn about self-care. Therapy became a turning point; it gave me the space to say things I couldn't say anywhere else. Eventually, I started to believe I was worthy of happiness, of healing, of building a new life.

Even the small things reminded me of how much had changed. One morning, not long after I moved, I woke up to a flat tire. There was no man in the house anymore to ask for help, and I had no idea how to change a tire. I knocked on a neighbor's door—someone I barely knew. When a snowstorm hit and I couldn't shovel the driveway, I had to ask for help again. Scott still cared. If I called, he would be there, but reaching out to him outside of parenting felt too painful, so I tried not to. It was all new, and all confusing. There were transitions I never even considered, moments that made me feel small, vulnerable, and uncertain.

Scott and I had a lot of hard conversations, arguments, and emotional breakdowns, but we tried to keep them away from Nichole. If something came up and she was nearby, we'd pause and revisit it later. Over time, it got easier. The intensity faded, and we didn't have to work so hard to communicate. It became more natural, more respectful.

Eventually, I started to forgive myself. I stopped fighting the truth of what I felt and began to accept it. I had made hard choices, and they caused pain, but I was doing the best I could. I started saying things like, "I am a good mother," and "I am a good person." It didn't come easily. I had to repeat it until I believed it. Over time, those words became real.

Simultaneously, Scott was also in therapy and working on himself. This made me so happy. This was truly when we started to evolve. We had to get through some very extreme feelings. Our therapists encouraged conversations with each other. We would have hard conversations, learning how to express emotions mindfully to achieve what was needed to push forward. We apologized to each other for many things from the past, and I needed that.

This was a time for both of us to start owning what had broken our marriage down, and a time for us to face those breakdowns together, put them behind us, and move forward, forgiving each other. Scott shared with me at one point that he had been very unhappy in our marriage and had thought about leaving. I never knew this, and it made me feel human, validated, and that I was not the only one.

Time doesn't erase the pain, but it gives you room to breathe. If you do the work, if you face it, feel it, and get help when you need it, you do begin to heal. Slowly, steadily, life starts to shift again, and one day, you realize you've made it through.

CONSIDER THIS SCENARIO:

Maybe one parent is going to Maine for the weekend, while the other is going to New Hampshire. The child says, I want to go with Dad this time; we can do something together next time. In a high-conflict divorce, that simple sentence can turn into a battleground. Consider that forcing a child to choose, or making them feel guilty for their choice, only adds to their pain. The structured agreements between parents are there for the adults. The children don't need the details. What they need is reassurance that both parents will continue to be there for them, no matter what. Is it really a problem to switch weekends because your children made a choice? Think about the depths of these situations and the forever outcomes they possess.

Our divorce was the most emotionally painful experience of our lives. The process felt like it lasted forever. I still carry parts of that trauma, especially in moments that bring it back. It changed who I was. I've learned that while adults may take years to heal, children often carry the scars silently and forever. PTSD from high-conflict divorce is real. It doesn't always look dramatic. Sometimes, it's a subtle withdrawal, a quiet worry about who's showing up or who's angry. Maybe they are putting up a front, too, not showing anyone their pain. That's why how we handle these moments matters so much.

My parents helped a lot with Nichole. They were the ones taking her to practices and school most days. What if Scott had insisted on enforcing strict schedules? What if I had done the same to him? That would have hurt her more than it helped us. We had to learn to let go, to let her decide, to make space for what felt right to her. Sometimes that meant swallowing our pride or stepping back from what felt "fair" to protect what mattered most—her peace.

When we were separating, Nichole had a friend whose parents were also separating and divorcing. They were constantly arguing, having massive fights and battling over their assets, custody . . . all of it. I can remember listening to her talk about it all and thinking, *There is no way I am doing that to Nichole; no way. The money, houses, cars—all of it means nothing to me when I compare it to her happiness.* Scott and

I would vow, even through all our pain, to not put our daughter through this. One day when Nichole's friend was over, she was crying so hard. The pain this poor kid experienced was heart-wrenching. Her parents just could not get it together enough to focus on her and her siblings. Their selfish, vindictive hate for each other was blowing their unit apart. I didn't know the family well, but listening to it was very sad. My heart hurt. At that time, I knew we would be different in every possible way we could be, and we were.

If you're in the thick of this, please don't wait. Try to find your version of therapy. Whether it's traditional counseling, or something more holistic like yoga, massage, acupuncture, reiki, or meditation, start somewhere. Just start something for yourself. There's no perfect path; the healing comes in the trying.

As hard as it all was, we kept showing up. We still had dinners together. We still sat in the stands at her games. Maybe not next to each other at first, but we were there, always. That never changed, and in time, we did start sitting together again. Like everything else, it evolved.

You just have to keep working at it.

I had moved into the new house, and we told Nichole she could be at either home whenever she wanted. It wasn't about dividing time equally; it was about making her feel comfortable. We made sure she knew she was welcome, wanted, and safe in both places. It all felt impossible, but because we kept her well-being at the center, it ended up being as okay as it could be.

There was a lot of sadness in that new house for me. I had gone from a home we built with our own hands to something, quieter and lonelier. We were separating incomes and dramatically changing our lifestyle. I worried constantly about what that would mean for our daughter, for me, for us. We stayed positive; we tried to make it feel normal.

When I finally started therapy, long after the divorce, I began the real work. It was harder because I had waited. I had to dig deep, reopening wounds I thought had already closed. Even now, some moments still feel raw. One moment that stays with me is the look on Scott's face when I told him I wanted a divorce. I still cry when I think about it. Hurting someone I loved was one of the hardest things I've ever done. Maybe that's why the friendship we have now means so much to me. It continues to heal what once felt broken beyond repair.

We never missed a game, and never missed an event. Nichole never had to scan the bleachers wondering if we'd shown up, or worse, if we'd fought and were missing. She got to just be a kid, play her sports, and know we were both there.

I watched friends go through divorces where the pain never healed. Weddings where one parent didn't come. Graduations where one sat in the back, refusing to be near the other. That kind of bitterness can cause so much damage. This parenting thing doesn't end when they turn eighteen; it's forever.

Sometimes, I wish I had screamed, cried, and felt it all more openly. The truth is, you can face your grief and still protect your child. The more you care for yourself, the better you show up for them. It's not weakness, it's love.

Healing takes time, it takes grace, it takes working together, even when it's hard. The peace it creates for your child is worth every ounce of effort.

My wish for you and yours is that you can build a foundation of cooperation and understanding, ensuring your child feels supported every step of the way.

xo,

Christina

JOURNAL MOMENT 5: Navigating Custody

Only when you feel ready, sit with your journal, find a quiet space, and take time with these questions. You don't have to answer them all. Just let them guide you toward what matters most right now, for you and your child. How will you get through this, with or without your partner? Some questions may not be relevant, or maybe you've already faced them, but they can still help you reflect. When you're ready, make an entry in your journal.

How are you currently caring for yourself during this transition?

Are your children already dividing their time between two homes, or is this change coming soon, if at all?

In the likely event of divided homes, will they be close to each other? If not, will the children be able to see both of you when they want?

How will you manage visitation?

Will you allow your children some autonomy in deciding where they stay?

If visitation has a courtordered schedule, will the children have some flexibility?

How will you and your ex work to keep them out of any conflicts?

If your child wants to see the other parent outside of the agreed schedule, will you be flexible?

How will your children's feelings be considered, will they have a voice?

What information do you truly need to share with them?

Which parent will the children stay with?

Have both parents sat together and discussed the whole process?

If this is not possible, how will you continue to plan custody in ways that are best for the children?

Are you prepared to answer their questions? How often can they see both of you?

Are your decisions truly in their best interest?

Do you need professional guidance to navigate this process?

What other ideas do you have from this reflection that you could journal?

Reflection Six: Planning Your Financial Future

PROMPT 6

Find a quiet space and, only when you feel ready, sit with your journal. Reflect on the boundaries you need to protect your emotional well-being during this transition. What conversations are off-limits? How can you create stability for yourself and your child?

IF EMOTIONS FEEL overwhelming, take a pause. One thing that helped me was mindful breathing. Just a few slow, deep breaths helped quiet the noise inside. It didn't fix everything, but it gave me a place to start when things felt out of control. Taking a few minutes each day to focus on your breath can bring calm and presence, especially during difficult moments.

I had just separated from Scott. I had bought a new house and car, trying to start over, but life had other plans. At the time of the divorce, I was working for a company I'd been loyal to for seven years. Without warning, they moved their operations to Miami. I had just closed on my new home, bought a new vehicle and now my job was ending.

The day my boss announced the closure was one of the most destabilizing moments of my life. I left the office in a fog, and on the drive home, I was rear-ended. My new car was demolished, and I remember looking up at the sky and whispering, "I am not going to break." I didn't know how I was going to survive that chapter. I had no tools, no guidebook. Meanwhile, the whole time, I was trying to portray that everything was going to be fine. How is it going to be fine? I'd just bought a new home, bought a new vehicle to get out of another very expensive one I could no longer afford, and lost my job! Ok? I mean, really!

Inside, I was collapsing. We had been financially comfortable during the marriage. We built that life from nothing. When everything we had built was suddenly divided in half, the change felt swift and brutal. The confidence I once had in my ability to provide disappeared overnight. I had to start again, and I had to hold it together for Nichole's sake. I did all I could to try and keep everything steady. I reminded myself that Scott was facing the same fears in his own way.

Managing finances after separation can feel like too much, but one thing was always clear: Children should never carry the weight of financial stress. The struggle may be real, but it's not theirs to hold. I did everything I could to protect Nichole from it. Stressing about money is something I have always loathed. When I was a child, I watched my parents struggle, working long hours to provide for us. When Scott and I first married, we were poor, barely making ends meet. There were times when we were trying to better ourselves in our careers and went without health insurance coverage. There were years during which we couldn't afford the dentist. I remember doing everything I could to make food stretch for as many meals as possible. Times were tough for many years. We both continued to work hard, often each having three jobs at a time, constantly crossing paths. One of us was always around for Nichole.

It wasn't easy. Moving from financial comfort to maintaining two separate households felt like losing the stability we had spent years building. I found myself remembering the early days, sharing one car, waking up at 3:30 a.m. to pack the baby into the backseat so I could drive Scott to work, just to keep the car for daycare, errands, and everything else. Those days of stretching every meal, making dark tuna and mayonnaise soup to get by, stayed with me. We had come so far from that life, and now it felt like we were slipping backward.

I reminded myself that we didn't lose everything. We adjusted, we cut back, and we lived with gratitude. Life could be worse; it was only money, only things. The luxuries faded, but the essentials stayed, and for that I felt grateful. After all, in many cases, that is more than some others have. Gratitude became my anchor: a quiet reminder that we still had more than enough.

Nichole was getting older, and it felt like the right time to teach her more about money anyway. Instead of just buying everything for back-to-school shopping, I gave her a budget. We made a plan together. It became something we could enjoy, while building the skills I hoped she'd carry with her. She met the moment with the same grace and gratitude she always had. She never threw tantrums. She always said thank you.

I remember once, when she was little, she asked why I couldn't just go to the ATM and get more money. Like many kids, she didn't yet understand that money had to be earned. So, I began teaching her. I gave her cash instead of using my card, let her feel the weight of choices, and allowed her to make her own small decisions. She learned early, and she learned well.

Scott and I never fought about money. We didn't go through lawyers. We agreed that Nichole's needs would always come first. If she needed something, we figured it out. We kept things quiet, and we remained respectful. People thought we were strange. They assumed something must be wrong with us for staying close and not turning against each other. What they didn't see was that we had already fought the hardest battles. They were buried deep within, and we were never going to make Nichole carry the cost.

After I lost my job, I hit the pavement fast. I updated my outdated resume, pushed through the fear, and went on

Me and my beautiful daughter 2021

interview after interview. Most of the time, I was told I didn't have enough education because I didn't have a degree. Competing with kids fresh out of college made me feel invisible, but I didn't stop. I found a job to keep the mortgage paid, and then I enrolled in college. I took on debt, and I made lots of mistakes. I slipped further into credit card debt trying to keep things going, but I kept moving. I was good with money. After all, I was in high levels of finance, overseeing millions of dollars. For some reason, during this time in my personal life, I just did what I had to so we could keep on with life. Honestly, I think I truly didn't care. There was so much to work through that money wasn't going to be the worst of it for me.

There were times when the sacrifices felt endless. I

stopped going out, I battled depression, I worked to keep my world small enough to manage. Some nights, staying home and not spending money was the only victory I had.

Normalcy didn't return for a long time. I faked it with fake smiles. I paid the most urgent bills and let others slide, doing my best to protect my credit. I acted like nothing had changed, but inside, I was drowning. Eventually, as part of my healing, I made it a goal to climb out of debt. I consolidated loans, I refinanced my home, and I chipped away at it, year after year, until I could breathe again.

Financial strain can shake everything you thought you had built, but it can also reveal how strong you've become. It taught me that survival is made of small choices, quiet sacrifices, and steady determination.

Looking back, the financial losses were real, but they didn't define us. What defined us was how we kept showing up. How we stayed in it together, even when it was hard. How we chose love and stability over blame and resentment.

We carried the fear, hoping Nichole wouldn't have to. That was our job, and I would do it all over again to give her the safety she deserved.

It helps to make a budget. Once I finally climbed out of debt, I lived by a budget so I could stay on track with my spending. One thing I was certain of was that I never wanted to dig a hole of debt for myself again. I did what I had to for survival, but digging out was hard. I wish I had started with a budget so I could better see my finances in front of me. Had I done that, I may not have dug myself in so deep. This is a perfect example of how emotions cloud one's judgment. I was a Chief Financial Officer, someone who understood money better than most, and I still messed it all up because it wasn't important to me in the moment. Emotions take control of just about everything. I wish I had known this sooner and recognized the need for support.

Are you and your former partner struggling with how to manage a new financial model? If so, how are you going to keep your children out of it? Don't let them feel guilty. Don't make them think you're giving things up because of them. Don't blame the other parent. The way you speak matters.

What you say can either feel kind and safe or mean and harmful. Ask yourself how much you really need to share. The truth is, very little. The more children are pulled into adult struggles, the more confused and burdened they become. Even adults struggle with money: children shouldn't be asked to hold that weight. They can still learn by budgeting, if taught gently and positively. These lessons can help them feel included in a healthy way.

If both parents deliver the same message, kids feel secure. When there's silence or contradiction, children feel lost. They try to figure out what's true on their own. It's hard enough for us, so imagine what it feels like for them.

I know a friend who could only communicate with her ex by email. Talking led to fights. Meeting in person was impossible. Surprisingly, they stayed committed to exchanging messages because it helped them stay aligned for the kids. They made it work, and you can too. Find the communication method that allows you to keep your child out of the middle.

Many adults carry deep wounds from financial struggles they witnessed as children. Think back to the hardest time in your life regarding money struggles. What it felt like to live with fear or instability. Would you want your child to carry that same weight? If not, then the message must be different. Even when life is hard, children need to hear something steady. Something that gives hope, not fear.

I've seen children suffer through financial battles that never should have touched them. I had a friend who constantly blamed her ex in front of the kids. Most of it wasn't even true. Her anger was so strong that expressing it became more important than the impact on her children. I tried to help her see what it was doing to them, but she couldn't let go of her need for revenge. Sharing too much, especially out of anger, can leave permanent damage. Unless a child is in danger, they deserve the freedom to love both parents without guilt.

We had to downsize and make big changes. How we explained it made all the difference. Consider the best way. Don't say, "We have to cut back because your father left us with nothing." Instead, say something like, "We're going to save a little right now." The goal was to keep Nichole from feeling trapped in a problem she couldn't fix.

I saw what happens when parents pull children into the middle. A friend of mine went through a divorce in which his former partner constantly brought the kids into financial arguments, telling them who wasn't paying, what they couldn't afford, and who was to blame. It wore the kids down. They didn't have the tools to carry that kind of betrayal. They ended up carrying guilt, confusion, and shame. None of which belonged to them.

Even when you do everything possible to shield your child from financial stress, they still feel it. Nichole would sometimes look at me and say, "It's okay, Mom," even though I hadn't said anything. Kids are intuitive. Consider the delivery of the message, and you will likely be good.

Money struggles are real. If you're in conflict with your former partner about finances, keep it between the two of you. Don't pass that stress on to your child. If you're facing something extreme, like losing your home, consider professional guidance.

The debt and financial shifts were terrifying. Working through them became part of my healing, one small choice at a time, one quiet sacrifice after another.

There were so many moments when it would have been easier to blame. To let the anger spill out in front of Nichole. I refused; I held the line. I reminded myself that this was mine to carry, not hers, and Scott did the same. Through all the pain, I'm most grateful that I never had to fight for him to be a good father. Often, people constantly fight each other in and out of court, constantly beat each other down, making it easier to give up on being a parent. Both of us wanted Nichole to have us in her life, equally and lovingly. We are both loving, caring parents. That didn't change because we were divorcing.

If you're in this place now, please remember that it's not weakness to seek help. It's not weakness to protect your child's emotional space. It's the strongest thing you can do. In time, when the dust settles, they will remember that safety you built around them, even when everything else felt like it was falling apart.

SCENARIO: KEEPING KIDS OUT OF FINANCIAL BATTLES

A friend of mine used to pick up his kids and hear, "Mom said we don't have money because you didn't pay child support. Can we go get cookies?" As hard as it was, he didn't argue or explain. He said, "Let's get the cookies, and I'll talk to Mom later." Then he'd call her privately. He never involved the kids, but their mom did. She told them everything, and it made them feel like they were being punished. Not to mention they were lies. He always paid his child support. My point is, he remained the bigger parent, not responding with the same unfavorable attitude, making the kids feel even worse.

When Scott and I divorced, we both made sacrifices to keep Nichole's life steady. We worked more; we spent less.

Vacations and luxuries became rarer, but we did our best to make her feel safe through all of it. When she wanted something we couldn't provide right away, we gave her the same message: "We're both working toward that, and soon it'll happen." No blame, no shame, just reassurance.

That first back-to-school shopping trip marked a shift. We had a tight budget. Scott and I agreed on an amount and made sure she heard the same thing from both of us. It was a big change from the past, when there weren't really limits. Nichole was never spoiled in a bad way; she adjusted, and she understood.

If money is tight, how you talk about it matters. Kids don't need to hear about child support or unpaid bills. They need to feel steady. You can be honest without adding fear. Instead of saying, "Your mother left us with nothing," try, "We're budgeting a little differently now, but we're going to be okay."

Even a small moment like saying, "I didn't get cookies this week, but I'll pick them up next time," can help teach that adjustments are normal. It removes the weight, and it helps them feel safe.

If money is tight, get on a budget as soon as you can. It helps you see exactly where you are and where to adjust. Over time, build an emergency fund, even if it's small. If possible, work with a financial advisor or explore debt consolidation. I took out a personal loan through my bank. It had a lower interest rate than the credit cards. We also had to cut way back; eating out, shopping, and yoga classes were now all luxuries, even though some felt necessary. So, I had to do my own yoga at home to keep it up. I know it sounds like I'm spoiled, but working to get where we were from nothing, then going back to the harder times, was tough. When necessary, remember there's no shame in using public resources like food stamps if it helps create more stability.

At the same time, use financial changes as a teaching opportunity. Don't pass down your stress, pass down your knowledge. When we went grocery shopping, I gave Nichole a small amount of money she could manage on her own. I only bought the essentials, but she got to buy something she wanted. It became a lesson: "Here's a dollar, let's see how far it goes." We made it fun, and that's how she learned—through experience, not fear.

Scott and I never discussed child support, bills, or financial concerns around Nichole. Those weren't her burdens. She didn't cause the divorce. She didn't need to carry the weight of our adjustment. Why would we make her?

We had shared custody, and as Nichole grew older, she had the freedom to choose where she wanted to be. That kind of freedom only worked because Scott and I communicated. Without that communication, things can become dangerous. I knew a couple who hated each other so much they never spoke. Their kids would say they were at one house but were really at a friend's or a party. That's not just rebellion; that's the fallout of silence, the lack of co-parenting.

Judges exist for a reason. When communication fails, courts help create structure. However, it doesn't always have to get that far. Imagine if custody were about cooperation, not competition. Imagine if divorce wasn't a battle to win, but a transition to navigate together.

We never let Nichole hear a bitter word about money. Even so, she picked up on our stress at times. Kids are perceptive; every word matters, as does every reaction, every sigh. They're always listening, even when you think they aren't.

You don't have to pretend everything is okay, but your child doesn't need to carry what you're going through. Say less when it helps them feel safe. Choose your words with care and let them stay kids for as long as they can.

THE TORNADO TUNNEL OF DIVORCE

People often pull their children into a tornado of anger. It's a storm so fierce and confusing that the kids have no way out. Sometimes, that storm is rooted in mental illness. Sometimes, it's raw pain. Either way, it becomes a whirlwind of emotion that doesn't belong to them. The truth is, if you're caught in that storm yourself, you can't shield them. You should work to heal. Remember, it is not just the two of you who are hurting; there is chaos around your children—a feeling of being trapped in something they never asked to be part of.

Most divorcing couples will, at some point, find themselves in that tornado. I was in it too. I questioned myself, and I wondered if I had made a mistake. Of course, Scott was hurting too. That pain is real; the confusion is real.

Show up for the games, the concerts, the ceremonies. Sit in the stands and allow them focus on their moment, not on the tension between their parents. They need to look up and see that everything's okay so they can go have fun. When they look up and see a parent missing, they might wonder, *Did my parents have a fight? Did I do something wrong? Maybe it is my fault they are fighting! What happened over the past few days that I might have caused?*

Try to find some sort of neutral ground for the sake of the kids.

I remember sitting in my living room one night, alone. Sitting with my thoughts and my confusion, fear, and loneliness. I had lost my job; I had no idea what tomorrow was going to bring. I started crying and couldn't stop. That night, I was pretty sure this was what rock bottom looked like.

I remember seeing the image of a tornado. It felt like it was calling me, like I could jump right into it and disappear forever. That was one of the lowest moments I've ever experienced. I sat with that sadness alone, but I didn't run and I didn't numb out. I stayed and kept fighting through. There was no way that tornado was sucking me in.

I had responsibilities. I had someone I loved more than

anything in the world to keep showing up for. That night, something shifted. I started to think about getting help. I knew I was at the bottom, and I knew I didn't want to stay there.

Even now, I'm grateful I didn't run toward the danger that showed up that night. It could have gone another way but didn't. Thank you for allowing me the space to share something so personal.

The hardest moments come when anger takes the wheel. I've seen what happens when one parent hates their ex so deeply, they stop caring how it impacts the children. They use fear, threats, and manipulation. Consider this: that kind of bitterness leads somewhere dark. It might feel like control now, but it can turn into loneliness later. Your children will grow up. They'll see more than you think. Eventually, they'll form their own opinions. They will be faced with more difficult decisions that they should not have to navigate, thinking, *I want a relationship with my mom (or dad), but I cannot take this hatred and control any longer.*

Processing emotions is necessary; we are all allowed to hurt. It's also our responsibility to protect our children from drowning. This is our divorce, not theirs.

Don't let your pain become the backdrop of their childhood. Don't spend every evening sitting on the couch, numbed out, sighing loud enough for them to feel it. Let them see you get up, and let them see you trying. I know it is not easy; fighting through emotion is exhausting. Keep going!

Don't spend your energy bashing your former partner and if they are doing that to you, try not to retaliate. That hurts them too much; they will appreciate the higher road someday. Try to redirect that energy to others and be more mindful of them. You love your children, or you would not be reading this book.

If your child says, "I miss Dad," that's not something to take personally. It's a need, and if it's safe and possible, maybe they should spend a little more time with him. If that's not an option, if the situation is more complicated, then reach out to someone who can help: a therapist, a counselor, someone who can help you find the best way forward.

Before you react, pause. Before you speak, breathe. Are the kids in the room? Can they hear you? Will your words make them feel supported, or more afraid? Is what you're about to say useful, or just reactive?

The reflections in this book are here to help you sort through it all. What are your roadblocks? What's making this feel impossible right now? Let's write it down, let's look at it clearly. Step by step, moment by moment, there's a way through.

It is perhaps a safe assumption to say that you and your partner are divorcing, but you are not divorcing your children, and they are not divorcing either of you. .

Someone I am very close to went through one of the roughest divorces I have ever been a part of. The constant pain of missing his children, and them missing him, was overwhelming. There was a brick wall of vicious revenge and rage in his way. He had years of trying to fight the fight, never once giving up on having a relationship with his kids. He always took the high road. He didn't bad-mouth his ex in front of the children. He kept quiet about the fight going on behind the scenes, and it was downright awful.

He possessed the true love of a parent, true dedication, and was always willing to consider the children, no matter how hard it got. It was a long stretch of struggle, constant setbacks, disappointments, and hope slipping away. He never gave up.

Eventually, his children grew old enough to make their own decision to live with him, and they began to see much of the truth on their own. Many years later, the children still longed for a relationship with their mother, but she was never able to heal. She couldn't let go of the hatred. It is a sad story because the children deserve a relationship with both parents. The only way forward in a situation like this is to stay hopeful that the mom can find her peace and someday reconcile with her children.

Sometimes the strongest thing you can do is say nothing at all.

There was a night, not long after our separation, when everything felt frayed. We were tired, trying to work through logistics, figuring out who would handle what. Finances were my strength and Scott's biggest trigger, so I chose to take the lead. Not because I wanted control, but because I wanted peace.

I sat down with a list: our home, our debt, our daughter. I asked myself, *What matters most? What would cause pain for him? What might weigh on Nichole?* I circled the things that didn't matter, then I let them go.

As I mentioned, we didn't hire two lawyers; we used one. That's right, we used the same lawyer, and I told her upfront, "I'm not here to destroy him. I want half the house, and I'll figure out the debt." She asked about the motorcycle and his business. I said, "I'm not interested in taking his livelihood or things that bring him joy." She pushed for more: child support, custody schedules, court orders. I said no. Nichole would see either of us whenever she wanted.

We were fortunate that we didn't need legal paperwork to guide our parenting. We were both invested, and that was what we needed. Remember, even if the other parent isn't cooperating, you can still take the lead. You can continue to press forward in a healthy manner, showing the children a safe path. We focused on stopping as much of the fighting as possible. Fights are usually fueled by the people in the fight. If someone decides to pull back, the fight will lose its strength.

I stayed quiet about what I could've fought for. Not because I was weak, but because I knew the cost. I wasn't going to turn our daughter's life into a battleground. I refused to make her pay for our pain.

There will always be people who say I should have taken

more and pushed harder, but they weren't there in the still-ness. They didn't see what restraint protected. They didn't see how silence created space for healing. Moreover, we likely would not have gotten to the beautiful place we are today had we fought each other.

This path isn't for everyone. If there's abuse, danger, or deep betrayal, your story will look different. However, if it's possible to let some things go, to choose calm over control, peace over punishment, it can change everything.

Sometimes, the kindest thing you can do for yourself and your child is to say nothing at all. Just quietly and clearly, choose love.

UNDERSTANDING NEEDS DURING DIVORCE: A MASLOW PERSPECTIVE

This reflection is about understanding our needs, too. Divorce shakes the foundation of our lives, and Maslow's Hierarchy of Needs helps explain why it feels so destabiliz-ing. At the base of the pyramid are our most basic needs: shelter, food, and safety. When a marriage ends, those needs often come under threat. Suddenly, there's a ques-tion of where you'll live, how you'll manage finances, how you'll keep everything together. It's not just emotional, it's survival.

Once those essentials are secure, the next layer comes into focus: love and belonging. Divorce fractures the very relationships we've built our lives around. That sense of connection, of having a partner, of being part of a family—it all shifts. You find yourself rebuilding that connection in new ways: through your children, through your friends, and sometimes through therapy. You need to fight for it. You need to rebuild that sense of belonging on your own terms.

Higher up the pyramid are esteem and self-actualization. These don't disappear, but they can get buried under the weight of starting over. You're trying to hold it together financially, emotionally, logistically, and somewhere in there, you're also asking: *Who am I now? What do I want from my life?* That's where self-worth, confidence, and personal fulfilment come in, slowly, layer by layer.

We don't always move through these levels in order. Life can pull you back to the bottom of the pyramid, but knowing what you and your children need can help you work your way back up. Consider taking one small step at a time.

My wish for you and your family is that you find the support and resources you need to get through the financial challenges of divorce, always with your child's well-being in mind.

xo,

Christina

JOURNAL MOMENT 6: Planning Finances

When you feel ready, sit with your journal, find a quiet space. Take time.. You don't have to answer every question: just let them guide you toward what matters most right now, for you and your child. Take a moment to reflect: How will you get through this, with or without your partner? Some may not ap-ply, or you may have already worked through them. That's okay. This is your space to reflect. When you're ready, write.

State one or more ways you are currently caring for yourself.

What kind of financial stress are you facing right now?

How is this stress making you feel?

What resources do you have available to navigate the stress of financial problems?

Do you need to make a budget?

Do you have resources to assist? If so, what are they?

How will you leave the children out of child support discussions?

How will you help the children cope with lifestyle changes that might need to be made?

Do you and your partner have the ability to unite and send the same message to the children so there's no confusion?

If not, what plans can you make to ensure messages remain safe and positive?

Do you need safety resources? You can find them online. For example, in Massachusetts Greater Boston Food Bank, SNAP Benefits, Emergency Shelters, Mass Health insurance. Check your states official website (e.g.statename.gov) for more resources.

Who can you reach out to?

Are your plans in the best interest of the children?

Will you need professional guidance through this process?

What other ideas do you have from this reflection that you could journal?

From left to Right: Scott, Nichole, my Dad, Tina, Mike, me, my Mom at my Dad's 80th birthday celebration in New Hampshire 2022

From left to right: My bonus son, my bonus daughter and my other bonus daughter, Mike and me at Thanksgiving 2022

Reflection Seven: Preparing for the Next Chapter

PROMPT 7

In this reflection, we focus on the importance of staying present, especially during moments of transition and stress, such as navigating the emotional ups and downs of divorce. Mindful walking can be a grounding tool to help you focus on the here and now, letting go of the overwhelming thoughts that often come with major life changes. It can be done inside or outside. Find a quiet space to walk and focus on each step. Pay attention to the sensation of your feet touching the ground. Breathe slowly and deeply. When your mind wanders, gently bring it back to your breath and your steps. How does this practice make you feel? Maybe journal about what came up.

MY STORY: HOW WE PARENTED TOGETHER, APART

HERE'S WHAT IT looked like to keep parenting together, even after we separated. When parents aren't aligned, kids feel it. They test boundaries and if they're already strug-gling, they need to know both parents are still on the same side.

It's also important to let your child just be while you stay flexible with each other. Call, check in, and adapt. Scott and I did this often. If Nichole wanted to change a plan or attend something different, we adjusted. Ask yourself: Are you letting your children have some choices, or are you clinging to something because it's "court-ordered" or you are angry with each other? That distinction matters.

It took us two years to reach a place where we could be in the same room without overwhelming pain. The look on Scott's face when I told him I wanted to separate never left me. Hurting someone you love deeply is its own kind of grief. I kept seeking forgiveness, and in that search, I found myself in some very dark places.

I've always considered myself strong, but the grief hit hard. The only way through was one moment at a time. Not a year, not a holiday, but just one small moment. Every time we had to show up together, I would pause. I'd sit in silence, I'd cry and sometimes scream. Oftentimes I would call my mom or my best friend and talk it through. Somehow, I had to face the sadness and guilt each time it surfaced.

I had to see Scott for Nichole, even though it reopened every wound.

Eventually, plowing through it all got a little easier. It took a long time, as well as consistent dedication to set my own feelings aside for Nichole and focus on what events were important to her. Today, when we gather as a family, I can look back and see the good. At the time, everything felt like a blur. Even as I write this book, I am making some guesses because it really was the worst time of my life. When you are experiencing these high emotions, you often unconsciously work to forget them all.

Even early on, we didn't miss anything in Nichole's life. We'd been *all-in* since she was born. We married young; I was 20 and Scott was 21. We both worked three jobs. If she had dance class, a concert, or a field trip, one of us was there, and often both of us, as we would leave work for a bit and go back. We were determined that divorce wouldn't change that.

Those early post-divorce years were hard. We both lost an unhealthy amount of weight, and we were both fighting depression. Each encounter re-opened the wounds. There were days I didn't want to go, but together, we went for her. Not for us, but always for her. Even if it meant driving to New Jersey for hours.

Nichole never had to look up in a crowd and wonder, *Where's my mom? Where's my dad?* She looked up, and we were there. Not always sitting together. Not pretending. We just stood by her side. Every concert, every holiday, every special occasion, even when it felt impossible. Of course, I was worried about his emotions, and I imagine he was prob-ably worried about mine. The guilt, the feelings of regret, all of it. We continually reminded ourselves, "She needs to see us both. She needs to feel *normal*."

Put yourself in their shoes. What does it feel like to wake up and not see one of your parents on Christmas morning? If you're separated by distance, consider staying at a hotel nearby. Figure it out. Ask yourself: *Am I making this about me, or about them?*

When one parent causes issues, kids start to wonder: *Will this ever stop? What is going to happen at my graduation? Will my wedding be ruined someday? Why do I have to choose? Why are my parents putting me in this position?* That's not fair to them. I know this first-hand because I have watched and continue to watch my bonus children go through this every day, to this day. After more than 17 years, their horrific divorce world continues. It is absolutely excruciating to watch children suffer in this way.

Court orders offer structure, but they're not written in stone. You can choose to rise above them if it offers more peace for your kids. If your child can't choose where to spend a holiday without fearing hurting one of you, then step in. Don't step in with control, but with kindness. Gauge who your child needs more in that moment if it cannot be both of you. Make it work; don't make them choose.

A cautionary tale: If you're thinking of moving away with your child, pause. Unless there's abuse, relocating can cause deep, lasting damage. I've seen it personally. A friend of mine faced a painful custody decision that left him with limited time with his children. The outcome caused deep strain for everyone involved. The court allowed his children to move states, believing their mother would have more support there. The result created distance no one could repair. For years after this, everyone would suffer. Kids suffer the most when they don't get enough time with both parents, even through the toughest times. They yearn for a relationship with both parents. In his case, unfortunately, none of the decisions were in the children's best interest. All of this because of a deep need for revenge that could have been avoided. It could have been done differently and resulted in his children having a healthier experience.

There are two roads: one that helps them heal and one that adds to the damage. Start small—sit in the same room. Share the same phone call. It doesn't have to be perfect. Birthdays, holidays, school events—they don't have to be stressful; they can be shared. **Co-parenting with grace** gives your child a sense of safety that lasts forever.

Think about what it looks like to be so bitter that you cannot be in the same room. Holidays would mean bouncing between houses, carrying stress, guilt, and pressure. Who would be hurt? Who would demand loyalty? This is what kids feel, and we didn't want that for Nichole.

And today, she never has to wonder.

We all go to everything together. Every birthday, every holiday. When my dad turned 80, we all went to New Hampshire. We wore matching T-shirts! It felt like a full-family celebration. Nichole invites both of us to everything, and she never has to choose.

I was at the salon one day, and the stylist told me about her divorced parents. She is such a sweet girl. She and her brother live in the middle of their parents' tension every single day. If they go to dinner with one, the other gets upset. *Why'd you go with your dad? When are you seeing me?* She said, "My parents need to read your book." That's the hope I have, to help children through the chaos that divorce can bring. To help parents find a common ground in co-parenting to support their children.

Nichole doesn't carry that weight. She can go to dinner with either of us, or both of us together. There's no score-keeping, no guilt, no shaming, just life filled with beautiful memories now, filled with love. For her last birthday, we even joked about who was going to "out-gift" who. In the end, we coordinated so we would give her the same amount. Still communicating, still in it together.

What is now? Now is not just for her, it's for us. We're friends—real friends. It's not forced; it just became true over time. We travel together; we go to dinner together. No kids, no awkwardness, just connection—something bigger than co-parenting now. It's genuine friendship and love; it is real. Some people are surprised, but for us, it works. It feels natural now, and nothing ever feels impossible. Friends invite everyone together, family invites us all, and nobody must choose. When I say all of us, I mean myself and my husband,

Scott and Tina. The four of us can go anywhere together, and we have created so many amazing memories.

It took time, a ton of time and a ton of new trust-building. If you keep your child's well-being as your north star, and let go of the bitterness, the possibilities are endless.

Our next trip is already planned, for just the four of us, and we can't wait.

Parenting together was never a battle for us when we were married. As with normal couples, I was the enforcer and Scott was the softie. Sure, there were sneaky scoops of ice cream Scott allowed before dinner when I said no, but we always aligned when it counted.

Even now, it's still: "How much are you putting in Nichole's birthday card?" We still coordinate, because it matters.

Some of those early holidays were a blur. We tried splitting time. Nichole would do one part with Scott's family, one part with mine. It felt so disjointed. So, we started doing things together again. Slowly, carefully. We were still hurting. Sometimes I resented how hard it was to stay kind. Over time, the more we showed up together, the easier it got.

One year, Nichole was going over to Scott's family for Christmas. I got to see her in the morning, but I did not see her until later that night. Christmas has always been my favorite: Santa, decorations, surprise presents, cookies and milk, all the tradition. When that changes, it leaves a deep emptiness. That day was one of the hardest I have ever dealt with. I was with family I loved, but it wasn't the same. I felt a deep loneliness, a loneliness nothing else could touch.

Now, we all do everything together. We are so grateful to have this beautiful, blended family.

When it came to Nichole, I knew early on that her feelings were important to us. Our job was to make her feel special, to encourage her to enjoy her time, and to let her know we couldn't wait to hear about all the fun she had. I kept my own feelings inside and let them out later, when she wasn't around. If I had told her how I really felt, she might have been afraid to share her happiness with me. I never wanted that.

Part of preparing for the next chapter is embracing new people. It is a gradual process, learning how to navigate new people in your child's life. Over time, I got to know Tina, Scott's new partner. When I saw that Nichole was safe and happy, I encouraged her to be discerning. If I hadn't liked Tina, it would still have been my role to allow Nichole to have her own opinions. Unless there is danger or abuse, children deserve a chance to build relationships with the new people in their parents' lives.

I also made a conscious choice not to introduce new partners to Nichole when I was dating. I knew when I was dating that I wasn't really into anyone. I was too independent, and I wasn't ready anyway. So why bring someone into her life if I knew I wasn't going to let them stay?

It is important to listen to your child when new people come into their lives. Support their feelings, and don't put your own emotions on them. Help them feel okay about the new person if it is the right thing to do.

Looking back now with honesty, if I knew then what I know today, I wouldn't have dated anyone for a long time after the divorce. It sounds cliché, but I would have run off, not literally, and spent more time finding myself. I would have worked harder on caring for myself. I think I would have been an even better support system for Nichole, and it might not have been such a struggle.

I was never jealous of Scott and Tina's relationship. I was glad he had support. Sometimes I felt sad seeing them do things I wish we'd done when we were married, but back then, we were just trying to survive and raise a child.

WORKING TOWARD SHARING EVENTS

Working toward sharing events is important. It shows that it's possible to maintain a calm, respectful space between co-parents and extended family. It reinforces something we don't hear enough: that shared moments and traditions can exist without jealousy, without tension.

I love that we can be playful together. We don't have to worry about stepping on feelings. There's no weirdness, no tiptoeing. We just are.

Scott and I still share a joke from the TV show *Friends;* all four of us are huge fans. We've seen every episode a million times. There's an episode where Monica and Rachel keep apologizing, and the neighbor just repeats, "OK" to annoy them. Scott and I still laugh about it.

We still use that joke. It's one of those little things that reminds me how far we've come. This morning, I texted to ask if they were going to breakfast. Scott replied, "Yes, we'll pick you up." I said thank you. His only response was, "OK."

It's those little things. The tiny moments that make this all feel normal, and simpler now. We hug each other like family, because that's what we are now. There's no jealousy, no awkward silences. Everyone knows where they stand and that security, that ease, is something I don't take for granted. It's a relief to co-parent like this. To be able to laugh, to be ourselves. It wasn't always this easy. It took so much healing, trusting, and foundation building, but it's truly bliss.

My hope is that you'll find your way to peace. That you'll show up fully, without fear or resentment, for the moments that matter most. Your child's well-being is always worth it.

xo,

Christina

JOURNAL MOMENT 7: The Next Chapter

When you feel ready, find a quiet space and sit with your journal. You don't have to answer every question. Let them gently guide you toward what matters most right now, for you and your child. Reflect on this: How will you get through this, with or without your partner? Some questions may not apply, or you may have already moved through them. Use what helps. When the time feels right, begin your journal entry.

Are you attending events for your child? Has your ex been there?

What would it look like to show up with peace rather than tension?

How are you managing your reactions during shared events?

Can you plan ahead for small moments of calm if things feel overwhelming?

Are you holding on to past hurt that makes these gatherings harder?

How can you begin to move forward?

What coping mechanisms do you practice or utilize at an event?

How can you shift emotions in a different direction?

How does it feel to see your ex again each time? Is it getting better with time?

Analyze the next event. How big is the room? How close will you be? What does this look like for you?

Are your plans in the best interest of the children?

Will you need professional guidance through this process?

What other ideas do you have from this reflection that you could journal?

Reflection Eight:
The Parenting Contract

PROMPT 8

While staying committed to the long-term promise of parenting together, it is also important to notice how this is affecting you emotionally. Co-parenting through divorce can stir up grief, frustration, and doubt, even when you are doing everything you can. Mindfulness can offer quiet support when things feel overwhelming. Try simple, grounding practices that help you stay steady as you keep showing up for your child.

WHEN YOUR CHILD was born or came into your life, you entered into an unspoken agreement: a quiet vow to protect, to guide, to keep showing up. That promise didn't end when your relationship did. Divorce might close one chapter, but the parenting partnership remains. Go back to that moment when you first held your baby in your arms. What did you promise them then? What will it take to keep that promise now?

From left to right: Mike, me, our daughter, Scott, Tina at our daughter's college graduation 2010

The day I discovered we were pregnant was a big surprise. We were both so young; we were nineteen and twenty. Just kids ourselves. When reality hit, it was the happiest day of my life. We didn't have much, but we poured everything we had into preparing for her. We stayed with it, even when it felt uncertain. That commitment gave us something to hold onto.

The pregnancy was rough. Morning sickness, anemia, toxemia, and back pain. I took it all as a sign that she was real, that she was growing. Every discomfort felt like part of becoming a mother.

Oh, let's not forget the mashed potatoes. I was up 65 pounds, craving mashed potatoes with butter and cream every night. Every single moment of discomfort was worth it to bring our daughter into this world.

Scott had cravings too. It made us laugh in those quiet moments at night. There was something comforting about sharing even the silly parts. It made us feel like we were doing this together. After dinner, later in the evening, I turned to my mashed potatoes, and he turned to a bowl of cereal or ice cream, trying to make an excuse for himself that the pregnancy cravings were rubbing off. It was a time of connection, the two of us anxiously awaiting our child's birth. Back then, it wasn't common to find out the baby's sex, so we didn't know. Waiting for that surprise gave us something joyful to hold onto together.

I remember the first time we held her. We made a quiet promise to love her without conditions, to keep her safe, and to provide for her as best we could. We meant it. We were so young, but in that moment, we were full of certainty. That promise felt simple and complete. It felt like forever. The key message is that she was born to BOTH of us forever and nothing was going to ever change that.

Unfortunately, the years that followed didn't go as we imagined. The ground beneath us shifted, slowly at first, then all at once.

The marriage was changing, and eventually, we separated. Still, the promise didn't dissolve with the relationship. It doesn't expire. It just had to take a new form. We had spent fifteen years parenting together, and now we had to figure out how to keep that same commitment without being a couple.

It wasn't easy. We were holding pain, fear, and regret. Sometimes we could barely look at each other without remembering everything we had lost. Even in the worst moments, we both kept coming back to that shared vow. Our devotion to Nichole mattered more than anything in the world. That became the thread we followed. The one thing we could hold onto that still felt true.

We reminded each other of it, especially when things were hard. Not with perfect grace, but with intention. Over time, something steadier began to form. It didn't look like a marriage; it looked like a parenting partnership. It was built slowly, choice by choice. Eventually, we created something that worked. Not just for Nichole, but for us too.

Nichole's high school graduation was one of the first large events we shared. It was 2006 and how could it possibly be that our little girl was graduating from high school and heading off to college? It was about two years after we separated, and things were still difficult. We still faced pain, anger, and sadness. There was no time for divorce feelings because our daughter's special day was the focus, as it should have been. We planned a nice party and all of us were there. It is quite remarkable when the love for your child can put all the hard feelings aside because they mean more to you than anything else in this world. We had a nice time, gleaming with pride. On the flip side, she was about to move out and go to college. On top of everything else we were facing, I was about to become an empty nester.

Nobody could have seen the tragic emotions of that coming! Off to college she went, living on campus, and I was in the house all alone, still trying to get back to feeling like socializing again.

The next year was rough, with another significant change to navigate. I started dating, and that is a story for a whole other book! I started getting together with friends more, and getting myself out of the house so I wasn't sitting in Nichole's room, crying that she was gone.

There were days when my ex and I could barely look at each other. The weight of resentment and disappointment sat between us. Yet even then, we knew we had to find a way through for her.

We were not okay, but this wasn't about us anymore. It was about keeping our word. So, how do you keep the parenting contract alive when the unit has been shattered?

I never really wanted to talk to anyone about the reasons I left our marriage. There is no easy way to express the details without people forming opinions and taking sides. My intent was never to make people hate Scott, so I just kept it all inside until I started therapy and literally unloaded it all. I remember an awkward moment in the beginning of the separation, when my mom asked me, "What happened?" My mom is one of my best friends in this whole world, but talking about the intimate details of my unhappiness over the years was never going to happen. She loves Scott like a son to this day, and I wasn't going to do anything to change that. Why would I? What would it accomplish, really, other than pain? I am not a vicious person. I would never do it; there was no point. My mom would never be able to understand the intimate details and quite frankly, she didn't have to. The simple answer was that we lost each other, grew apart over the years, and there is much truth in that, so it is what I stuck with.

You do it by remembering what matters most. Not your pride, not being right, no blaming, just keeping the focus on the child who still needs *both* of you to show up. Unless there is truly an unsafe situation, the children deserve both of you, the same way they did when they first entered this world.

We started talking, about just small things at first. Checking in, meeting up, little by little. We found a way to be around each other without it feeling like we were reopening the wound. Eventually, we could talk like people again, not exes. Just two people committed to the same child. The resentment shifted over time through our own individual healing. Each of us did our own work, letting go, forgiving, and healing.

We realized we weren't broken. We were just different now, and different doesn't mean worse. It just means it takes more effort and more grace.

When I think back to that day in the hospital, holding Nichole, I can still feel it. That overwhelming love. That instinct to protect her from everything. So, during the divorce, I kept going back to that feeling. I had to remind myself that none of this changed how I loved her. If that was true, then nothing changed about the promises I made. Scott felt the same way; he is an amazing father. That mutual commitment is what allowed us to grow.

Nichole and I spent a day together recently. She's grown now, and is responsible, kind, and everything we hoped she'd be. Whenever I am around her, I still cannot believe how the time has passed us by.

We are still her parents, still holding true to the contract. Still showing up with love. That instinct to protect her never left, even though she's grown. The promise we made is still alive. It is steady, sacred, and lifelong.

It took the same sacrifices we were always willing to make. The same energy, the same focus. It became about keeping our feelings in check, about not letting our emotions get in the way of her peace.

I've watched so many friends go through divorce, and I know they felt the same way I did when they first held their babies. However, somewhere along the way, the pain took over and they lost themselves (mostly unintentionally) in their emotions. This was when their kids suffered the most.

You don't have to let that happen. You can still keep those promises. It's hard work, but it's worth it. It takes steady dedication to your love for your children. Pushing through the hardest moments, doing the uncomfortable work, choosing not to take the easier road, and returning again and again to the one that asks more of you.

If your ex makes that kind of communication impossible, your choices still matter. I had a close friend go through a brutal divorce. His ex was filled with hatred, doing anything she could to hurt him, even in front of the kids. It was heartbreaking. Yet, he never wavered. He stayed focused. He never spoke badly about her. He kept showing up; he stayed committed to the same love he always had for his children, since the day he held them for the first time. Now, as the kids have grown, they've maintained a strong relationship with him. Sadly, however, they're still trying to find that connection with their mom.

I still remember holding Nichole for the first time, thinking, *This is it. I'm here forever.* No matter what changes around us, that promise doesn't end. On a Sunday morning at 6 a.m., my contractions started. They were far apart. The day moved slowly, and we didn't arrive at the hospital until around 3 p.m. Everything continued at a crawl. Then, at 5:20 on Monday evening, nearly 36 hours later, a beautiful, healthy baby girl came into our lives. In that moment, we could never have dreamed of loving another human more, and we were right.

Imagine the future. See yourself at every milestone: graduations, weddings, birthdays, baby showers. See yourself there. See the life you can still share with your child, even if you're no longer sharing it with your ex.

Your child is still yours; that promise didn't end. Everything you vowed the day they were born still stands. It still matters, they still need both of you to be there. You can do this . . . you absolutely can.

Maybe divorce doesn't end a family. Maybe it simply changes how the family holds together.

In the beginning, I didn't know how we would do it. Seeing Scott felt like being hit by everything we had lost. The silence between us wasn't neutral. It was full of tension, unfinished conversations, and things neither of us could say without hurting the other. Underneath all of that was one shared truth: we both loved Nichole, and we both knew she didn't deserve to carry any of it.

We didn't get it right away. There were times when I was so upset I had to take deep breaths just to walk into the same room. Times when I wanted to let my emotions win, but I didn't. I made a choice, again and again, to protect her peace instead of feeding my anger.

I kept telling myself the same thing: *This isn't about me, this is about her.* I promised her I'd always show up. That commitment didn't end with the divorce; it became more important than ever.

There were long stretches where showing up meant doing the emotional work quietly. Talking to friends, going to therapy. Learning how to sit with sadness without placing blame.

The one person I could talk to in detail was my best friend Becky. She is the only person on this earth who knows everything about me that I know about myself. She listens without judgement; she never judged Scott, no mat-ter what. She would never hate him; she just understood that sometimes marriages do not work out. She knew what I went through over the years and just listened and sup-ported every decision I made. It is what we do for each other; it is what makes us the best friends we have been for more than 40 years now. She helped me talk things out, offering encouragement and constantly reminding me how much I loved Nichole. One Sunday morning, I was sitting on my bed at around 7 a.m., exhausted from a continual lack of sleep. I honestly cannot even remember why I was so angry with Scott that morning; I just remember that I was so mad, I could barely see straight.

I felt as if I were spiraling out of control, thinking about heading over to his house and causing a scene. Unable to control my thoughts, I felt disorganized, like I could do something irrational that I would later regret. In the early hours, I paced back and forth in my room, screaming and crying. I knew I had to call my best friend; otherwise, I might end up on the front page of the local newspaper, looking like a crazy person. She calmed me; she asked all the right questions. She reminded me who I was, what kind of per-son I am, what my focus and intentions were, and the fact that I'd vowed to get through this divorce without this kind of stuff happening. I will always be grateful for her uncon-ditional friendship, her loving, caring nurture, and her guidance. We have both helped each other through some of the toughest times. I thank God for her every day.

Sometimes, it meant saying nothing when I wanted to say everything. That was hard, but we kept going.

Over time, something softened. We talked more, we coordinated better, we were finally discovering a new way. Eventually, we started to rebuild trust. Not the trust of marriage, but the trust of two people choosing to raise their child with respect.

It still amazes me how far we've come. Scott, Tina, Mike, and I have shared so much over the years. We travel together; we sit around dinner tables and laugh.

Two of my greatest pleasures from this tragic breakup have been Tina and Mike coming into our lives. Tina came first, about three years before Mike. Tina is truly a gift from God; she is literally my soul-sister. Who would have thought that our divorce would result in one of the most beautiful friendships of my life? A friendship we will share and treasure forever. A friendship with my ex-husband's wife . . . what? It took a bit to get here, that's for sure. Both of us were leery of becoming friends because that is what society tells us. Friends with the ex's spouse? It's not normal for most people, but for us, it is very normal. What I love most is that Nichole has another special woman in her life, someone who loves her very much and would do anything for her.

Along comes Mike. Scott and I have known Mike since we were kids, because he was my brother's best friend in high school and after. In the beginning, Scott was really upset because we promised we would not date anyone from "the circle." I didn't really consider Mike a part of our circle because he was more in my brother's circle, but Scott struggled for a while with us dating. After a few months, he started to see what I saw—a good man, a good father, and someone who was taking very good care of me and loving me. For the first time since we divorced, I had a man in my life who would measure up to both of our expectations. Mike and Scott started to form a bond like Tina and I did, and they are now best friends as well. I know it all sounds so odd, but it works for us, and it works for our daughter. We have so much fun together and we always mention our dynamic when we are out to eat or at an event. People cannot wrap their heads around it. Most people think it's great though, and have always told us we should share our unique story . . . so here we are.

Back in 2007, a very close friend of ours tragically passed away in a construction accident. He was one of our best friends and the pain of losing him forever was unbearable for all of us. These are the times that so much gets put into perspective. After we got through the gruelling process of his burial, we decided to hold a fundraiser for the two children he left behind. We formed a committee and created a trust fund for his children. Scott, other friends, and I were on the committee. We all met regularly and held a very successful fund-raising event. There were more than 500 motorcyclists. We all met together at a local store parking lot and took a police-escorted ride together to a lake our friend used to frequent. We had a memorial ceremony there and all rode back to a club where we celebrated his life with bands, food, friends, family, and love. This was a huge turning point for us all, realizing that life is too short to be wrapped up forever in pain and emotions. The four of us were ready to start the next chapter of our lives, together and in harmony, and so we did.

There is no pretending, no tension—simply the family we've chosen to become. It didn't happen overnight, but it happened because we never stopped choosing Nichole.

There were moments Nichole would call and say, "Can we all go to dinner?" and we would. No tension, no choosing sides. Just us, showing up again and again. I didn't realize how powerful those small choices were until years later, when she told me she never felt caught in the middle.

Even when new people came into the picture, the standard stayed the same. Show up, be kind, stay consistent. That's what children remember. They remember who stood beside them.

You don't have to get everything right to co-parent well. You just need to keep your promise and keep showing up with intention.

The vow you made when they were born.

The one that says, *I will love you more than I love my pride.*

If you can do that, everything else becomes possible.

Ask yourself:

Are you putting your child's well-being above your pain?

Are you building a future where they feel safe, loved, and free of guilt?

That's the real work, and if you stay with it, the rewards can be transformative for your child, your family, and even for you.

My wish for you and your family is that you stay committed to the parenting promise you made the day your child was born and continue to support their well-being through every chapter.

xo,

Christina

It was extremely difficult to navigate any hatred that surfaced. I have loved Scott since I was 16 years old. However, there were plenty of times that hatred surfaced, and it was hard to fight off. Trying to be sympathetic was much easier than hating. For some reason, in this case, I was really upset. I remember sitting on my couch crying, wanting to lash out, wanting to retaliate. I opened my phone and started a text message to Scott. There wasn't anything good about this idea. Instead, I called my best friend and talked it out. Sometimes the choices we make can influence better outcomes.

JOURNAL MOMENT 8: The Parenting Contract

When you feel ready, find a quiet space and sit with your journal. You don't have to answer every question. Let them gently guide you toward what matters most right now, for you and your child. Reflect on this: How will you get through this, with or without your partner? Some questions may not apply, or you may have already moved through them. Use what helps. When the time feels right, begin your journal entry.

State one or more ways you are currently caring for yourself.

Can you take a moment to think back to the day your children were born?

How did you feel the first time you held them?

Can you acknowledge your commitment to the parenting contract?

What kind of conscious promises did you make to them?

Did you promise to keep them safe, show them love support?

Will you be able to maintain this commitment through the divorce?

What are some roadblocks you are facing?

How will you break through them?

Will you show up regardless of how difficult it gets?

Is there anything you can say to your ex to remind them how they feel about their love for your children?

Is it possible for you to get together and have a coffee to talk? Maybe it's not and that's ok. You can still maintain your own commitment.

Do you need to reach out to someone for support? Who will you reach out to?

Are your plans in the best interest of the children?

Will you need professional guidance through this process?

What other ideas do you have from this reflection that you could journal?

Reflection Nine:
Prioritizing Self-Care

PROMPT 9

Nutrition is a very important part of self-care. Make time to eat mindfully. Nourish your body with foods that fuel you, not just fill you. Slow down, notice each bite. Pay attention to how your body feels as you eat, and what it needs more of. Let meals become moments of calm, not just tasks to get through. This small pause can help you reconnect with your body and ease some of the stress you're carrying.

THE WORST TIME OF MY LIFE

I DIDN'T HAVE the knowledge or education I have now when I was going through the worst time of my life: my divorce. I knew some things about self-care, but not like I know today through education. Things would have been so different for me had I focused on this more. I want people to be able to do this work earlier, to support themselves before the pain takes hold the way it did for me. At that time, I was twenty pounds underweight. You could see my ribcage. My face was drawn; I had dark rings under my eyes. It looked like I was dying, and that was certainly how I felt.

I lost a lot of friends. Most of them had been mutual with Scott and me, and after the separation, they pulled away. Some turned on me—people I never guessed would do this. I honestly feel that they just didn't understand, and that isolation made the grief even heavier.

My best friend stuck by me; she was my rock. She let me talk; she let me vent with no judgment. She came over in her pajamas, sat with me, and never once tried to push me to do something I wasn't ready for. She always met me where I was. She was the one who talked me down from the ledges. Looking back, I don't know what I would've done without her.

That same year, dating was a disaster. My bestie used to say, "I'm so glad we're done dating," and I finally understood what she meant. I was meeting men on online dating sites, and what a catastrophe of continued events! When we met in person, I would park my car blocks away, just to feel safe. I never used my real name until I trusted someone. I thought any decent man would respect that. Most of the time, the dates were disappointing.

One man stood me up at a restaurant. We had agreed to meet at the same chain, but in different towns. I showed up on time and waited, surrounded by the 5 p.m. construction workers who started joking with me that I'd been stood up. When he finally called, he was angry, asking where I was. I asked him the same. As you might suspect, he'd gone to the wrong location. He apologized and said he'd come to me, but I told him not to bother. It was a red flag, and I didn't want to ignore those anymore.

Another time, the man looked nothing like his profile photo. We had zero chemistry, and when the bill came, he said, "I thought these days, girls paid the bill." That was it for me; I was done. It is not that I mind paying a bill, but I am somewhat old-fashioned and still enjoy a little chivalry. So, not on the first date!

I realized I didn't need a man in my life. I had been Scott's wife and Nichole's mom for so long, and I loved those roles, but I had never just been Christina. So, I decided to intentionally take a full year off from dating and figure myself out. It turned out to be one of the best years of my life.

It was 2006, and I was 39. Then I turned 40, and everything hit me at once. I felt like I wasn't where I wanted to be. I didn't recognize my life, and nothing felt settled or safe. It was a strange mix of growth and grief, but I kept going. My 40th birthday came around. Now, I am someone who loves my birthdays to linger for weeks. I love to feel celebrated and spoiled. Not this year! I told everyone I knew that they had better not even think about a 40th birthday party for me. I didn't want anything to do with this birthday. I never pictured myself divorced, alone, starting over financially, with so many new roadblocks to overcome at 40! Are you kidding me?! My sweet mom asked me if we could do something, anything, together for my birthday. She took a few of my closest friends, herself, and me on a Boston dinner cruise. It was perfect actually, very low key—just what I needed.

That year taught me something important. I had spent most of my life giving to others. I finally saw that I couldn't keep doing that without giving to myself. Like they say on airplanes, I had to put my oxygen mask on first. I had to stop waiting for someone else to save me. It needed to start with me.

MY STORY: THE PROCESS OF REBUILDING

Divorce isn't just the end of a marriage; it's the beginning of a long, often painful process of rebuilding. For so long, I focused on making sure everyone else was okay: Scott, Nichole, and our families. I never truly checked in with myself, and when I did, I realized that the emotional weight was crushing. I thought I could power through, but I wasn't coping very well at all, and I was barely surviving. I didn't realize I had to do something until I reached a breaking point. Therapy changed everything for me. It gave me the tools to process my emotions, to stop blaming myself, and to start focusing on what I needed to heal. I also learned that self-care isn't selfish, it's necessary.

Whether it was therapy, journaling, or simply taking walks to clear my head, I had to find ways to nurture myself through the pain. One morning, I woke up and felt so much anger that I was out of control. I stepped into my backyard and screamed into the open air, screaming, screaming, screaming out loud. It felt so good, and I realized this was a new therapeutic tool for me. It released so much anxiety. Whatever works for you, even the silliest things, do them. I am sure that if anyone saw me screaming into the woods in my backyard, they might think I need to be committed. But each time I did it, I felt better, and that was a great thing.

As I kept doing these screaming sessions, something shifted. I began to smile, and then I laughed, on purpose—loud, exaggerated laughter that helped move the energy from anger to relief. It might sound strange, but it worked.

I wrote the passage below in 2006, shortly after I started therapy. At the time, I felt like I was drowning in grief, guilt, and life. I didn't know where I would end up, only that I had to keep pushing forward. Looking back, I can see how deeply I was still in survival mode, fighting to reach a place of peace. If you're in that place now, I hope these words remind you that survival can still lead to peace.

Her peace

"I am the waves in the ocean crashing on the beach. I am powerful yet calming and relaxing. I rise and build strength as I find my way back to shore, where I am peaceful. The very tides of my existence continually try to pull me into the deep sea, where there is a world of unknown and fear. It is a place where I could disappear and get lost forever. I continue to fight my way back to the shore where

the crashing waves surrender to calmness and peace. My process is continual, strong yet graceful. I am grateful for my strength and beauty. My dedication to my journey and destination is admirable, a loyalty not all possess. Peace and tranquillity are at the shore. I work hard to be there. I love who I am."

That first summer after everything fell apart, I started gardening. I had no idea what I was doing, but something about it felt grounding. I planted vegetables, watched them grow, and felt proud when I picked them. It was simple, but it gave me a sense of peace.

The next year, I tried again, but nothing came. The garden failed, and for a moment, so did my hope. I had done everything the same, but nothing grew. I almost gave up, but instead, I started learning. I found out that at our new home, there weren't enough bees for pollination. The problem wasn't me; the problem was the environment. That changed how I saw everything. The moral of this story is not to give up on anything. When you are feeling low, it is so easy to feel like you are failing, or to ask, "Why is everything happening to me?"

That experience changed a lot for me. Sometimes, the tools that help us one year stop working the next. It doesn't mean we're failing. It just means we need to learn something new. Healing is like that. You try something and it works, then it doesn't. You adjust; you keep going. Something always grows again if you stick with it and don't give up. So, don't give up on yourself.

If you're unsure, start by exploring different options. Go online and find things that interest you. For me, it was difficult too. I didn't know how to channel the energy that was consuming me. I didn't want to go out with friends, I didn't want to date, and I didn't want distractions. I was lucky though, because after about a year, I realized my outlet was education.

I started studying nutrition not long after. I wanted to give back, so I earned my bachelor's degree in dietetics and later studied at the Institute for Integrative Nutrition. That education helped me get my body back on track after a cancer scare.

It was time—time to care for myself in a way I never had before. I quit smoking cigarettes after 20-plus years in 2009. The scare of a spot on my lung was what finally made me quit. I promised myself I would never smoke again if it wasn't cancer, and luckily it wasn't. From there, I started an education path that inspired me to care for myself more.

During that time, I also did deep retrospective work, including breathwork. I found one of my purposes in that process. I redirected all the energy that once made me smoke, twisted my stomach in knots, triggered anxiety, and even made me feel suicidal. Therapy was my first step, and through that, I discovered my passion for helping people. I wanted to be a leader in some way, and that journey led me back to school.

Divorce wasn't just an end; it was a collapse. I had spent so many years trying to hold everything together that when it finally broke, I didn't know how to function. I was always the one making sure everyone else was okay, sacrificing my well-being to keep the peace. Watching Scott in so much pain, knowing I was the cause, was unbearable. I wasn't just dealing with my own emotions; I was carrying his, and naturally Nichole's as well.

At first, I wasn't coping. I spiraled, barely getting through each day. I put on a strong face for everyone around me, but deep down, I was completely falling apart. I isolated myself, avoiding friends and family, convincing myself that I would be a burden if I let them in. Some days, I barely had the strength to get out of bed. When Nichole came home, I'd splash cold water on my face, take a deep breath, and pretend I was okay. I wanted her to see me as strong, even when I felt like I was breaking. Now, I know and understand better that being vulnerable is also strength. You don't have to carry it all. You just need to keep showing up with honesty to yourself.

I finally found a therapist I connected with, and that was when things started to change. She helped me see that I wasn't responsible for Scott's pain and validated that I was going through my own. I had been so focused on being the strong one, on keeping things moving forward, that I had never given myself permission to grieve what I had lost.

Slowly, I started focusing on myself for the first time in

years. I threw myself into taking long walks in the woods, races, and even a triathlon. I trained for it alone, competed alone, and finished it alone. It was the first time I accomplished something physical like that, just for me.

I started my education after my divorce, so I knew nothing about taking care of myself during that time. The worst of it lasted two years. The hardest part about self-care is that it's not a one-size-fits-all approach. It's about helping each person identify what soothes them and what works for their individual needs. I was searching for inner peace, trying to begin a wellness journey I didn't yet understand. I used to criticize people who said they were "working on finding themselves." I had that "get-over-it" mindset. Well, when I hit that place, I thought, *I need to run off and find myself because I am insanely lost here.* So, I began.

Losing my job led me to a new career because my company moved to Miami and I didn't follow it. That's when I realized I needed an education. I was rejected from so many jobs because I didn't have a degree. Taking the business role at the psychiatric hospital was an opportunity I never would have pursued otherwise. The hospital administrator believed in me and hired me as an assistant administrator. This, paired with pursuing my master's degree, is what led me to where I am now. She told me I had a way about me that was meant to serve people, and she took a chance on me. I proved myself, and here I am, the administrator of a treatment center.

It was my certification from the Institute for Integrative Nutrition as a Holistic Health Coach that pushed me into the highest level of self-care. This was when I learned so much, building a long list of tools to help me feel more grounded. I was able to truly start practicing meditation and spirituality. Before that, I was just working with my therapist on healing, but this was next level.

I was journaling daily, practicing gratitude, waking up to a morning meditation, and going to sleep with an evening meditation. It was a slow, evolving process, figuring out what worked and what I connected to. For example, I truly couldn't meditate for years. I kept practicing with guided meditations even though it was hard for me, because I'm very sensitive to people's voices.

Like in the scene in *Eat, Pray, Love* in India, where Julia Roberts is sitting in a meditation room. She leaves it super frustrated, and when asked what was wrong, she talked about how she could not focus; all she could think about was how she would decorate her own meditation room. This was me. I was so distracted with my thoughts that meditation felt impossible. I just kept doing the work, returning to my breath each time my mind took over. Eventually, with practice, I got better and better. Guided meditations really helped. I still use them at bedtime and for my morning gratitude, to set my day.

Perseverance, a constant desire to make change, carried me through. I knew I couldn't stay in the spiral I was in forever. Friends and family helped, being honest with me about my state, helping me see myself. My therapist helped me realize how I was spiraling, suffering, and even self-sabotaging.

This was the year I really started my self-awareness and self-care. For the first time, it was just me. I had no man, Nichole was in college, and Scott had Tina. It was just me. Time to grab the reins and start focusing on myself for the first time in my life. I was always my parents' daughter, Scott's wife, Nichole's mom. Now I was just me. I started the journey of truly loving myself during that year.

That's something I can't completely remember. However, looking back, I think I moved from acceptance to resentment, and then back to acceptance. From the beginning, I tried to be accepting of what Scott was going through. Then it turned to resentment because I felt like nobody was acknowledging my pain. Later, I found acceptance again, once Scott started to accept the realities too. We went back and forth many times, and that seems normal to me now. I was in so much pain that sometimes it hurt that the focus was on Scott's pain. Just because I was the one who left, it didn't mean it was easy for me.

That year of being a little more "selfish" turned out to be one of the most important years of my life. I realized that being me was enough.

The timeline went something like this: I separated in 2003 and divorced in 2004. That same year, I started therapy. In 2007, I began studying dietetics, and by 2013, I had earned my bachelor's degree. I became a Certified Holistic Health Coach through the Institute for Integrative Nutrition in 2016, and later a Certified Family Recovery Coach in 2019. I completed my master's degree in 2022, and I achieved my LADC-I in 2024. The year I took off for myself was 2006. The reason for these dates is to show you that it takes time. There is no deadline; just work slowly and achieve when you achieve. No pressure . . . there is enough of that naturally in divorce.

Forgiveness was the key to my recreation. I was able to turn my anger toward friends and family, whom I felt had abandoned me, into a more sympathetic way of thinking. Later, I learned that our divorce was hard on everyone. Family and friends didn't know what to do. Some had known us as a couple for years, and suddenly, that was gone. Shifting my mindset to being more loving instead of angry was how I finally started to forgive. I really didn't consider the impact our divorce had on those closest to us.

As some of our other friends divorced, I started to understand how sad it is from the outside: finding yourself in an awkward situation when you were hosting events and didn't know which person to invite. To this day, we have divorced couples as friends who were never able to get into the same space. It is still difficult to sort out. We invite both and leave it up to them to decide, but it really stinks when you want to see both people.

Today, I feel so much gratitude for us, for our ability to co-exist. Our initial focus was Nichole, but now our friends and family value our ability to show up for everyone and together, even though we are no longer married. All the hard work has paid off on so many levels. It is the peace we were all searching for.

Looking back, I can see the mistakes I made in those early years. I thought I had to do it all alone, but now I know I should have leaned on people more. I should have let my family and friends in instead of shutting them out. I was afraid they would take sides, that they would hate Scott, that they would pity me. I didn't want to be the one everyone felt sorry for.

What Scott and I built after our divorce is something I will always be proud of. We put Nichole first, and over time, we created something that still feels like family. We travel together; we share birthdays and holidays. We show up for each other, even now. It isn't perfect, but it's real, and it's built on love, respect, and hard work.

If you're in the middle of it right now, I hope you know this: you don't have to do it alone. You don't have to hold it all together. Let yourself fall apart if you need to. Let others in if it feels right. Take care of your body, your mind, and your spirit. You are more than your role in the family; you are a whole person who deserves to heal.

Let's go back to that year I took off. I needed space, real space. So, I stopped dating, asked my friends to stop setting me up, and took a true year off.

Ironically, just as I was coming out of that year in late 2007, I reconnected with my now-husband. We had known each other as kids. Life sure has a funny way of working out. In those moments, I had no idea what was coming next. Each step kept putting me on a better path, even though I couldn't see it while it was happening. That was when I started building a relationship with the Universe and with my spirit, trusting that something bigger was guiding me, even when I felt lost. It was a gift I couldn't recognize until it unfolded right in front of me.

During our initial separation, one relationship lasted a little over a year. It is a funny story how we met. He cut me off on the highway, and a week later, he found me at Starbucks. He came up and asked, "Are you the girl from the highway? I wanted to find you again. We're meant to have dinner." He seemed normal, so we started dating. We had fun together, but deep down, I knew he wasn't my forever. I wasn't ready to love anyone else. I was still carrying so much guilt, feeling like I had broken up my family.

Eventually, I sat him down and told him the truth. I said, "You're my rebound. I need some space. My head's not in the right place." It hurt him, and it hurt me too. After that, I dated a few more people, but nothing felt right. That's when I took the whole year off. I realized that dating was just distracting me from the real work I needed to do on myself.

After Scott and I split up and I started dating again, it felt like I was purposely finding all the wrong men. I had one disaster after another. I started to think that men my age were nuts. That is why I took the year off for myself; I was done. No more men, thank you.

Honestly, looking back now, if I had known then what I know today, I wouldn't have dated anyone for a long time after the divorce. It sounds cliché, but I would have run off (not literally) and spent more time finding myself. I would have worked harder on caring for myself.

MEDITATION

Meditation did not come easily to me. For years, I tried to sit still and tried to clear my mind, but I always felt restless. I would hear people talk about how transformative it was, but for me, it just felt frustrating.

Then in 2019, I was offered a chance to attend a leadership retreat in the Catskills. My manager couldn't go, and asked if I'd like to take her place. I said yes not knowing how much it would change me. For four days, we meditated, practiced yoga, and spent an entire day in silence.

At first, I struggled. My thoughts raced. I kept thinking about work, about my to-do list, about everything except what was in front of me. Still, somewhere in the quiet, something shifted. I found my breath, I found stillness, and I found a kind of calm I had never experienced before.

I came home from that retreat with a new commitment

to myself. Even now, I take short meditation breaks during the day. I put up a sign that says, "Come back in five," and I sit quietly with my breath. It is a small act, but it keeps me grounded.

It does not have to be meditation. Find whatever works for you. It could be gardening, running, or anything that connects deeply with your soul. The goal is to heal, to resonate, and to feel spiritually aligned, light, and powerful. I try to do something every night before bed. I use the Insight Timer app and fall asleep to guided meditation.

In the summer of 2022, I had been in my new role as administrator for a year, and I was drowning. The facility needed major restructuring, and once again, I had taken on everything myself. I wasn't sleeping, I wasn't asking for help, and the stress caught up with me fast. As I mentioned, I ended up in the hospital with severe colitis and eventually had to undergo a colectomy. It was a wake-up call.

That medical leave gave me something I hadn't had in years: space to reflect. I was ready to walk away from my job completely. My husband, steady as ever, said something that stuck with me. He told me to take a month and write down everything I could change before making a final decision. I did, and it changed everything. I realized that most of the stress I was experiencing was due to my inability to delegate and let go of everything. In other words, it was mostly all within my control to change it. So, I started making in-depth plans of change for when I returned from the medical leave. In divorce, part of self-healing and self-awareness is recognizing what is within your control and making change.

During one hospital stay, I had a roommate who was there for her third surgery. She felt extremely anxious. The nurses kept trying to calm her with medication, but her adrenaline was winning. She kept apologizing to me because she was crying and breathing heavily. I got out of bed, walked over to the curtain, and asked if I could enter. She welcomed me into her space. I stood by her feet and told her to breathe, to look at me, to breathe with me. I rubbed her feet gently through her hospital socks, made eye contact, and guided her through deep, slow breathwork. Eventually, she calmed down and slipped into a restful sleep.

When she woke up, she thanked me again and again. She kept saying, "You have a gift." She told me that nothing else had helped her the way that moment did. It reminded me why I do this work. Helping others grounds me. It gives me a sense of purpose I cannot explain. Something to consider through the deep emotions of divorce is to find your purpose. There might be many things that come to mind, many things that make you feel good. Go with them, embrace them.

After nearly three months away, I returned to work and changed everything I could. One major change was delegating the after-hours calls I had been taking. I reassigned them to my amazing team, and they were happy to assist.

I also addressed the people who had become intrusive in my personal time. Some would call while I was on the treadmill and expect me to stop. One of the biggest shifts I made was setting boundaries. I started telling people, "I have to be able to put you through to voicemail." Surprisingly, they understood.

Even with all the education I had, I still needed to turn to others for help. Through retreats, hypnosis, or breathwork, I needed guidance. I am so grateful I sought it. Now, I love my job. Four years later, I am still there, working alongside one of the best teams I have ever known.

MIRROR WORK:

Mirror work helped me love myself again. It helped me start turning my negative thoughts to positive. Working on how I saw myself after everything I had been through was extremely challenging. I had spent so many years self-sabotaging and suffering from guilt. It made me feel more confident as I moved through the healing process. My therapist introduced me to this model, and I honestly couldn't believe how effective it became. At first, it is hard to do mirror work. When I started, I saw a woman who had broken up her family and felt like a failure. Over time, after doing the work regularly, I started to see the beauty in myself. I am a good person—loving, caring, and supportive. Today, I still speak positive affirmations into the mirror when I am putting on my makeup or brushing my teeth. I am intentional about seeing myself and telling myself how wonderful of a woman I am. It is an excellent healing tool and should be used carefully, mindfully, and maybe even with some guidance from a professional, so it yields a positive outcome.

THE 12-MINUTE DRIVE

Stress has always taken an unbelievable toll on my body. It raises my blood pressure, blocks my ability to maintain a healthy weight, triggers headaches, body aches, and neck pain. Sometimes it feels like my whole body is crashing. I've learned that I need ways to release it, or it stays with me and wears me down. For me, driving through the forest on my way home became a kind of meditation, a small but powerful transition from the weight of the day to the peace of coming home.

One day, I was driving out of work, up a small hill where I could see the facility shrinking in the rearview mirror. I remember deliberately noticing it. I chose to look at it, acknowledge it, and leave it behind. In that moment, I realized I had an opportunity. I could either carry the stress of the day with me, or I could let it stay there as I moved forward toward home, dinner with my husband, my happy puppy waiting for me, and the life I am building outside of work.

That drive through the forest became part of my self-care without me even planning it. I drive the same road every day, through the trees, past lakes and streams, sometimes catching glimpses of deer along the way. I silence my phone. I make a conscious effort to see the beauty around me. Some days, the water sparkles through the trees. Other days, the leaves dance across the road. Even just noticing a patch of sunlight breaking through the branches reminds me there is always something good to look for.

Before I leave the forest, I also make myself acknowledge one positive thing that happened that day. Even on the hardest days, there is always something. A small moment of laughter, a patient helped, a challenge overcome. I take it with me like a little stone in my pocket.

By the time I reach the other side, I'm lighter. The stress isn't completely gone, but it's loosened its grip on me. I call my husband. I start shifting into home, into family, into being present. Without that reset, I know the stress would follow me inside, slipping into my evening, my sleep, my life.

There is still plenty of stress in this role, even after hours. Therefore, finding ways to cope, redirect, process, and release is how I survive it.

Visualization has become a part of this too. Sometimes I picture myself leaving the stress behind, like it's falling off me onto the road. Other times, I imagine pulling calmness into my body with every breath. It sounds small, but it changes everything. When you do breathwork, it can help to state, "breath in positive, blow out negative," or something similar.

If the forest isn't your place, find somewhere that is. It

could be a short walk, a song that moves you, a few minutes sitting with your journal or a coffee. It doesn't have to be big; make it your own. Find something that helps you brush off the day and shift into something softer, something kinder, for yourself and for the people you love.

NUTRITION

When I was going through the worst of it, I couldn't eat at all. I lived on wine, coffee, and cigarettes. I was underweight, exhausted, and barely functioning. I was falling apart.

As I moved to the next stage, stress eating became my default. After everything I learned in my education, I finally understood why. Binge Eating Disorder (BED) is a brain-based illness, not a failure of character. Learning about BED changed everything because I identified that I was suffering from it.

One Sunday, I spent the entire day bingeing. Full meals, then more, bread, cookies, chips and dip, cheese and crackers, cake, brownies, pizza, or Chinese takeout. I ate until I felt sick. I was alone in the house, and no one was there to stop me. It didn't matter how full I was; I kept craving more. I had no self-control. The next morning, I had gained six pounds overnight. I felt ashamed. I lashed out at myself for what I had done. These are signs of BED, and I worked with my therapist to face it.

That was the moment I knew something had to change. I started working with my therapist, learning how to manage the urges. I stopped restricting the foods I love, because that always backfired. I started using a food tracker, not to control myself but to stay mindful. I try not to numb out with food anymore; I try to listen to what my body really needs. There are still times I face a binge or stress-eat at work. I don't berate myself anymore. I just acknowledge where I am and work to get through it.

Later, I learned how to eat better and how to teach others to do the same. I even taught classes on how to eat healthy on a tight budget. Nutrition matters, not in a perfectionist way, but in a loving, aware way. When you feed your body well, you give yourself a better chance to face what life throws at you.

MY SELF-CARE FOCUS AREAS

1. **Stress Management:** Meditation, Yoga, time for myself, breathwork, time at the spa.
2. **Spirit:** Trusting the universe, God, gratitude, journaling.
3. **Exercise:** Long walks with my dog, strength training, Pelton, 5K charity walks.
4. **Nutrition:** Food tracking, food prep, cooking with my husband with love, shopping at my favorite farm stand, slowly chewing and tasting each flavor.
5. **Sleep:** Supplements, meditation, limiting screen time before bed.

CREATE YOUR OWN WELLNESS SPACE

What did you determine is your therapy? Maybe it is a combination of a therapist, a garden, a long walk, a candlelight bath, yoga, and meditation. Whatever it is, can you start to practice more regularly? Can you get some combination of your therapy in each day? Even if only for a few minutes? What about nutrition? Are you feeding your body well? What changes can you make to start a new lifestyle? Maybe use a nutrition app to start tracking your food? Maybe start with one or two days of healthy eating, then keep building? Spirituality, exercise, nutrition—whatever it is, you deserve it. Start slow; this is YOUR wellness space. It is for you; it is your journey.

Caring for yourself can feel extremely overwhelming, but it is important. Start slow, and don't beat yourself up over it. Don't use words like "failure," and be sure to find wellness things you love. You will have a much better chance at sticking with something if you love it and it feels easy to embrace. If not, if it feels like just another burden, you won't want to stick with it.

My life is unbelievably busy! I don't have a ton of time, so I want to spend it doing self-care that I love. I don't have time for anything else, and it cannot feel like another job to me. If I commit to something and don't feel like doing it that day, I simply don't. I don't beat myself up;, I just go with what feels right to me. My biggest commitment to myself is to do something I love each day that contributes to my well-being. It changes with my mood, and that is perfect.

I recommend you Google a Wellness Wheel assessment. There are a few of them available; find one that speaks to you. It is a great exercise and one you will do many times, because it will change for you as time passes and you continue to heal. It will also help you prioritize where to work the most on yourself.

Search for guided meditations for sleep, stress, and gratitude. There are apps you can download, but also lots of YouTube videos. Watch for the ones that are commercial-free because there is nothing worse than a commercial barging in on you when you go deep into meditation.

Search for fitness apps and videos. There are tons of YouTube workouts, and there are sure to be a few that speak to you. Plus, there are so many to match the amount of time you have.

I strongly recommend finding a nutrition-tracking tool. Many fitness apps have a free version that is good enough to track how well you are fueling your body.

My wish is that you'll care for yourself in ways that speak to you. Not out of fear, but out of love. You have people who need you, and *you* also need you. I hope this is the beginning of a healing journey for you, something you can build upon and continue to practice.

xo,

Christina

JOURNAL MOMENT 9: Self Care

When you feel ready, find a quiet space and sit with your journal. You don't have to answer every question. Let them gently guide you toward what matters most right now, for you and your child. Reflect on this: How will you get through this, with or without your partner? Some questions may not apply, or you may have already moved through them. Use what helps. When the time feels right, begin your journal entry.

The University of Colorado Boulder has a wellness questionnaire that I really like. What I love most is that you can keep coming back to it. Your answers won't always be the same, and that's the point. You grow, you shift, and this tool helps you see where you need to focus. Just Google wellness questionnaire and find one that feels right to you. There are plenty out there, and they're a great way to check in with yourself and figure out where to start.

When you're starting your nutrition journey, please don't deprive yourself of the foods you love. That never worked for me. It just led to bingeing, and we've already talked about how that spiral can go. Try not to even use the word "diet." For me, that word came with years of disappointment and guilt. Lifestyle changes are what stick. Pick one small, healthy change at a time and make it part of your routine. Just one.

And don't take away the things you love. If you love pizza, have pizza. Maybe the change is having it less often or not overdoing it. I'll have mine with a salad and veggies, so I'm not tempted to eat the whole pie. And if there's leftover pizza, I give it away. Because if it's in the house, I'll keep picking at it. That's just how I am.

You don't have to overhaul everything overnight. Just take little steps. Do what feels good. It shouldn't make your life more stressful. This is about support. It's about feeling better, not worse.

And eating healthy on a budget? That's no joke. You can buy a box of Twinkies for the same price as two or three organic apples. But here's a trick I like. Take those apples, chop them up, add a little butter and some crushed crackers or oats, bake until they're golden. Just like that, you've got five or six sweet little treats. It's way better than a Twinkie, and your body will thank you.

Can you take a moment to check in with how you are feeling right now: guilty, angry, hopeful?

What kind of support do you need today? How do you think it could help?

Are there any old behaviors that no longer serve you or your children that you're ready to let go of?

Can you list one or two healthy boundaries you would like to put in place moving forward?

What does inner peace look like for you today?

How can you start to accept your circumstances while still taking steps toward something better?

How can you communicate more effectively?

How can you bring moments of joy into each day?

How can you avoid arguments with your ex today? Can you acknowledge their feelings too?

List some positive affirmations you can feel.

What unhealthy labelling might be showing up, whether intentional or not?

Can you sit with your breath and observe changes?

Can you create a prayer for letting go of some things or to move forward?

Can you set some healthy boundaries you can return to when things feel uncertain?

What does your higher power mean to you?

What kind of support do you need right now?

How do you think the support will help today?

How do you ground yourself (a walk, a swim, a massage, yoga)? Can you invite your children to join you in some of these?

How are you coping with your feelings? Your child's feelings?

Can you create your own self-care regimen?

What other ideas do you have from this reflection that you could journal?

Reflection Ten:
Introducing a New Partner

PROMPT 10

Mindful Journaling: Take a few quiet moments to check in with yourself before writing. Reflect on how you're feeling about the process of introducing a new partner to your children, whether in your life or your former partner's. Notice any emotions that surface, such as fear, guilt, hope, anger, or anxiety, and let them come without judgment. Write with intention. Let your thoughts flow honestly and gently. This simple practice can help calm the mind and bring more clarity as you move forward.

OVER MY PROCESS, I was living two completely different realities at the same time. This part of my story highlights two extremes. On one side, I was working my butt off to support Nichole in her acceptance of Tina. I encouraged their relationship and made sure Nichole felt safe enough to open her heart to another woman in her life. I wanted her to know that no matter what, I was her mom, a great mom, and that would never change. How beautiful it could be to have another mom-type role model. Over the years, Nichole built a beautiful relationship with Tina. If I had portrayed any sort of jealous rage, it would have made it much more difficult for Nichole to embrace a relationship with Tina. I truly had complete control over how that was going to move forward. Today, she calls Tina her "bonus mom," and she acknowledges her on birthdays, Mother's Day, and all the special days. It makes me proud to see that.

Of course, it is natural to feel threatened by a new person that your ex-partner is introducing into the family circle, especially in the case of infidelity. Having the confidence to allow this to take its natural course is not easy. I remember the first time Nichole referred to Tina as her "bonus mom," not her stepmom. She did this through a beautiful plaque she got Tina for her birthday that had the definition of a *bonus mom* on it.

Even though I had consciously supported the relationship, I still felt a little threatened. Understanding this was a great time for self-reflection, a time to turn this feeling of threat into pride. After all, this was about Nichole, not me. Nichole felt good about this next level of feelings for Tina, or she would not have bought her such a nice sign with a world of expressive emotion written all over it. That should have made me happy, not feel threatened. In that moment, I felt a little tearful inside as I was able to see the beauty in the gesture.

From left to right: Nichole, me, Tina in Ireland 2022

On the flip side, I was facing a completely different situation with my current husband's children. The experience was a constant challenge. I spent years trying to build trust with his kids, only to have it broken down again and again. Every time I pushed forward even a little, it felt like I got beaten back twice as hard. It wasn't until the kids grew older and were able to form their own opinions that my efforts started to finally make an impact. It took years. Today, I am so grateful to have the relationships we fought so hard for. Through my current husband, I gained a bonus son, two bonus daughters, and a bonus granddaughter. More beauty added to our blended family.

Out of respect for my husband and our kids, divulging too much detail is not what I want to do here. However, if the walls could talk to you, the story would be more than you could fathom. For me, as a loving mother, I wanted a relationship with his kids so badly. Fighting for this was exhausting, but I stayed with it. Again, I focused on keeping my emotions in check, never bad-mouthing anyone. Eventually, the children came to their own conclusions and let me into their lives. It took years of patience and remaining kind, keeping my instinctual reactions in check, and leading with kindness and compassion versus revenge and retaliation.

When is the right time to introduce a new partner? How do you protect your child's heart without letting your own fears get in the way? Timing, communication, and intention matter so much.

I remember sitting at a family cookout during the early stages of my relationship with Mike. His kids were there, and they were still so young. I had already spent time with them a few times, but it was always complicated. All I ever wanted was for them to feel safe and loved during one of the hardest times in their lives. As a mom, I kept reminding myself that they were still adjusting to the fact that their parents were no longer together.

I didn't know how I was ever going to fit into that dynamic. On one side, I was welcoming Tina into our family life, trying to build something functional with Scott. On the other, I was trying to make something work that clearly wasn't being supported. I wasn't truly welcome. The kids were too young to understand.

I kept trying to meet Mike's kids where they were emotionally; I never rushed them, and I didn't judge. I just kept showing up with patience, with love, and with as much grace as I could manage. I had to work hard not to internalize the pain, even when it felt personal.

It was never about me. It was about their well-being. I knew in time, as they grew older, they would form their own opinions. Slowly, over many years, we built a relationship. Today, I am close to my bonus kids, and I am grateful for the connection we share. It means everything to me.

The time came for Nichole to meet Tina. I knew that as a parent, I had a lot of influence over how she would feel about this new person in her life. I remember watching the movie *Stepmom* with Julia Roberts and Susan Sarandon, which has a scene I'll never forget. Susan Sarandon's character is riding horses with her kids, and her son turns to her and says, "Mom, if you want me to hate her, I will." That moment hit me. In my story, I was both Julia and Susan. I was the mom encouraging my daughter to embrace someone new, and I was the new woman being rejected. I saw both sides firsthand.

Nichole needed me to allow her to like Tina. I could see the worry on her face. She didn't want to hurt me. She needed my permission to form a bond with Tina.

It was never about us; it was always about the kids. They don't want conflict. They want to love the people in their lives without guilt. Sometimes, the conflict isn't even real. We create it, and we pass it on. You can choose to sabotage it all, but it is likely not going away. For the sake of the children, if they are safe, why not allow them to move forward?

When Scott started dating Tina, I felt a strange kind of relief. Maybe this would help. Maybe someone else could help balance some of the emotions, could be there for him in ways I couldn't anymore. I wanted to encourage Nichole to build a relationship with Tina, not to replace me but to show her that moving forward could be okay. That life could still hold good things.

Luckily for all of us, Tina turned out to be exactly the balance we needed. She was good to Scott, and she was good to Nichole. She was accepting, kind, and real. In time, she became my best friend.

Like everything in life—friendships, family, or work—you have a choice. You can build bridges, or you can break them down. I've always been a relationship builder. Even when everything around me was shifting, I shifted too. Building trust, one patient step at a time. That's how we all evolved, together.

It wasn't always easy; it wasn't always fair. I believe choosing connection, even when it hurt, shaped who I became as a mother, a bonus mom, and a person. Love doesn't get smaller when it's shared; it grows. Sometimes the bravest thing we can do for our children is to show them that.

MY STORY: MORE ABOUT MY CURRENT HUSBAND AND ME

As I mentioned, I've lived two extremes of divorce. I was the mom who had to give her child permission to love another woman, and I was the woman who needed that same kind of permission from someone else. The two experiences unfolded completely differently, and the impact of that difference was profound.

With Scott and Tina, the story was built on patience, trust, and encouragement. Scott began dating Tina shortly after our separation. Nichole was around sixteen when she met her for the first time. I remember asking her how it went. She said, "Yeah, she's alright ... I don't know." I could tell she was testing the waters, trying to read my face, making sure she wouldn't hurt me. She barely knew Tina, but she could sense something was changing. I told her, "Maybe next time you see her, talk to her about what you enjoy. Share something about yourself. See what happens."

That was the moment I realized just how much influence I carried. My reaction could either give Nichole the freedom to open her heart or make her feel guilty for even trying. I wanted her to feel free. Over time, she built a beautiful relationship with Tina. Watching that bond grow is still one of the proudest experiences of my life.

When I met Mike, I carried that same hope into our life together. I thought we could build something healthy with his kids, too. I believed that even if things were hard at first, we would work through it. After all, look at what we had achieved with Tina and Scott. Surely, with patience and kindness, it would happen again.

There were times I questioned everything. I'd sit in my car, staring out the window, thinking, *What the hell am I doing?* It wasn't just hard, it was soul-shaking. After all I had been through over the years with my own divorce, the horribleness of dating, and being on an amazing road to my own healing, I questioned taking all of this on.

There were so many moments when I wasn't sure we would make it through, but we did. I had just been through so much pain, and Mike's divorce was just beginning. I had done so much work on myself, gotten all my confidence back. I knew I was a great catch. I was still young, attractive, with a solid career, and I owned my own home. Why would I ever want to get wrapped up in even more pain than I had already spent so many years healing from? Why would I want to deliberately dive into a huge mess? I saw it coming and walked toward it anyway.

Despite the agony and heartache, I stayed, even though every ounce of my soul was telling me to walk away. I am happy I did though, because now, we share such an amazing relationship. We have so much in common. We have fun together and we love our family. After several years together, we finally got married. I am grateful every single day that we held on.

It took years to undo the damage that had been done.

Years of showing up, staying steady, loving those kids from a distance when that was all I could do. I wanted so badly to have a relationship with them from the very beginning, but the influence of anger and resentment ran deep. It wasn't about me, and it wasn't even about Mike. It was about pain being passed down in the only way some people know how, by hurting others.

I kept telling myself: "Control what you can control. Stay the bigger person, even when it feels impossible. Trust the universe. It's not easy. but it works."

Children are looking to us for how to feel about the people in their lives. If I had made Nichole feel guilty about liking Tina, would she have built that bond? Probably not. If I had reacted to Mike's situation filled with hatred, with more hatred of my own, would I have relationships with my bonus kids today? Probably not.

The kids see it; they feel it. They gravitate to the people who make them feel safe and loved. Staying calm, being kind, taking the long view—it mattered. Even if it took years, it mattered.

I remember early in my relationship with Mike, thinking I could jump right into his family's life. That we could all be one big, blended family without all the pain. I was so wrong. That mistake taught me one of the biggest lessons of my life: You cannot control other people; you can only control yourself: your reactions, your emotions, your delivery.

There was a time at work when that lesson saved me

too. I was on a Teams call with my staff, going in with good intentions. I wanted them to feel involved, valued, and part of the bigger picture. Somehow, the meeting turned, and they started telling me they felt unsupported. They were attacking me, and my first instinct was to react, to defend myself. However, I caught myself. I breathed, I empathized, I listened. Because of that, the conversation shifted. Instead of leaving that call hurt and angry, they left feeling heard. That is the power of emotional control. It changes outcomes.

Life kept throwing challenges at us, and it still does. Every single time, I try to remember I have the power to choose how I respond. Nobody controls me but me. It took a long time to get here, a lot of therapy, a lot of nights doubting myself, a lot of faith in the universe that if I stayed true to kindness and love, it would come back to me.

After a long break from dating, I ran into Mike when I least expected it. I had finally stopped searching, and there he was. I didn't think I would ever marry again. Divorce had left such deep scars. However, healing opens doors you don't even know are there. Trusting the future instead of fearing it—that's what made love possible again.

I'm stronger now than I've ever been. I have more faith in myself, more peace in my heart, more trust in the unfolding of life.

Looking back, everything really did happen for a reason. If I hadn't divorced Scott, I never would have met Tina.

She became a major part of my life, encouraging me when I doubted myself, helping me through some of my hardest times. She believed in me when I was still struggling to believe in myself. That's right, one of my biggest life influencers is my ex-husband's wife. What do you think about that?! She encouraged me to go back to school; she has always been a huge supporter. I mean, really, who would have ever thought!

My relationship with Scott changed, too. He's one of my best friends now. I love him deeply, without stress or conflict. It's a different kind of love. A bigger, more peaceful kind. What do you think about that one? Seriously, I never, ever thought we would be here. I never imagined this could all become the reality we live in today, the beautiful life we all share, the beautiful memories we build together. Never in my wildest dreams!

Getting here wasn't easy for any of us. Therapy helped me finally believe that self-care wasn't selfish; it was essential. That my well-being mattered, not just for me, but for Nichole too. It took two years to fully accept that truth. If I could give you one gift, it would be not waiting that long.

Mike and I spent many years together before he proposed. It happened on an ordinary night, getting ready to go to dinner with Scott and Tina. We were running late, and I was rushing him. He asked me to turn the kitchen light back on, and when I did, he was on one knee. "Christina, will you marry me?" he asked. I said yes. The first people we shared the news with were Scott and Tina, two of our best friends.

We got married in 2021, with about forty of our close family members and friends, who all gathered at an Italian restaurant. One of our dear friends served as our justice of the peace. It wasn't fancy, it wasn't elaborate. It was perfect. We got married in the back of the restaurant in the garden area, then shared great food and spirits with our closest people.

This blended family we have now, with all its scars and all its healing, is one of the greatest gifts of my life. Every day, I'm grateful for it. Every day, I'm grateful for the woman I became along the way.

My wish for you and yours is that you will embrace or introduce a new partner in a mindful and accepting manner, always prioritizing the well-being of your child.

xo,

Christina

JOURNAL MOMENT 10: New Partner

When you feel ready, find a quiet space and sit with your journal. You don't have to answer every question. Let them gently guide you toward what matters most right now, for you and your child. Reflect on this: How will you get through this, with or without your partner? Some questions may not apply, or you may have already moved through them. Use what helps. When the time feels right, begin your journal entry.

State one or more ways you are currently caring for yourself.

If you have already introduced someone new to the family unit, take some time to journal about it.

Do you have a new person in your life that you want the children to meet?

Does your former partner have a new person in their life that they want the children to meet?

Has enough time passed for this introduction?

Do both of you have a plan to deliver this news mindfully? If not, will you be able to deliver this news alone? Do you need someone else for support?

In any case, will the children be able to form their own opinions?

How will you cope with your children having a potential relationship with someone new?

Can you both support new relationships without making the children feel guilty?

Are you prepared to support them if they are struggling with a new person being introduced?

Are your plans in the best interest of the children?

Will you need professional guidance through this process?

What other ideas do you have from this reflection that you could journal?

Reflection Eleven: Protecting Children in Divorce

PROMPT 11

Get your journal ready. Practicing gratitude, even during the hardest co-parenting moments, can gently shift your mindset from frustration to appreciation. Try to acknowledge the good moments, the love your child receives, the small signs of progress, the times you managed to stay grounded. Writing down just a few things you're grateful for each day can help create a more positive, emotionally secure space for you and your children.

EVEN WITH THE best intentions, certain choices can leave lasting emotional wounds and even cause PTSD. It's important to recognize the common pitfalls and learn how to avoid them, so that your children continue to feel emotionally secure. Some studies have shown that as high as 39% of children involved in high conflict divorces suffer from PTSD or Post-Divorce Trauma.

From left to right: Tina and me on an outdoor walk together 2023

I met Mike about four years after Scott and I divorced. Scott and I had made it through the toughest times, and Nichole was finally becoming safer from it all. She was off to college, and Tina and I were starting to build the early stages of our friendship.

Not everyone will be as fortunate as Scott and I were. Sometimes one parent wants peace, and the other refuses to allow it. Remember, even then, the parent who wants peace will likely have the strongest influence on the children. It will pay off. Even if it doesn't seem like it at the time, the children will see it, and they will appreciate your efforts someday. Trust me, I know. I have seen it firsthand.

What I also learned is that not caring for yourself along the way can cause damage all around you. That old saying is true: You are only as good for others as you are for yourself.

The very focus on continuing to parent Nichole with the love and commitment we always had is what kept us moving forward. I've said it before, but Nichole is truly the reason we are where we are today. If we had divorced without a child, maybe we would have stayed friends, or maybe not. In the beginning, there was so much resentment and pain that it would have been easier to walk away.

One thing is certain: Nichole held us all together. She helped us keep loving her more than we hurt. She made us pause and think: *Are we helping her feel safe, or are we adding to the hurt?*

When you go through a divorce, it's easy to get caught up in your own pain. It's easy to want revenge. Stop and ask yourself: How far will you go to hurt your ex, and what will it do to your children?

I have witnessed extreme situations among friends and family. Situations where the need for revenge hurt the children the most. I know of a mother who has three children, and none of them speak to her today because of the emotional damage she caused during the divorce. The hatred she carried became their burden. When they grew up, they chose to walk away, not from her ex, but from her. This hurts them; *of course* they want a relationship with both of their parents. Unfortunately, she forced them into a decision they wish they didn't have to make. It feels so unfair to them.

Children see the truth with time, and they gravitate

toward stability. They recognize manipulation, even if they don't have the words for it yet. When they do, it will force them to make painful decisions that could create abandonment. These decisions are unfair because children yearn for healthy relationships with their parents. That's why healing is so important. If you don't let go of hatred, if you let it fester inside you, it doesn't just hurt your ex, but risks hurting your children, possibly even causing long-term emotional scars like PTSD, which affects many children in high-conflict divorces.

I remember sitting on my bed so many nights, alone and scared, with nothing but my thoughts for company, and they were not positive thoughts. They were filled with guilt, regret, and confusion, all of it swirling with no clear way out. They were filled with resentment and anger.

From the outside, it had looked like we had everything. A beautiful home. A strong family. Scott was certainly a wonderful man, and I was a wonderful woman. Yet, there I was, questioning everything. *Why did it go wrong? Why couldn't I fix it? Why couldn't I keep the family together? Why did I feel I had to leave? Why couldn't I just stay?*

I didn't realize it then, but I was drowning in guilt, and that guilt kept me stuck, unable to truly grieve or heal. It was a lonely, dark time. I felt myself slipping toward rock bottom. I couldn't eat; I didn't want to see anyone. My naturally social personality had all but disappeared. I couldn't even look in the mirror without feeling shame. I didn't recognize myself anymore.

At the time, I thought healing was just about survival. Over and over, I had to remind myself that it was never just about me. It was about protecting Nichole, too. Staying stuck in guilt and darkness would have touched her life, no matter how hard I tried to hide it. Children feel everything we carry. Even when we think we're shielding them, they absorb it.

Healing gave me the strength to show up for her. More calm, grounded, and loving. It gave her the emotional freedom she deserved, and a mother who was whole enough to love without passing on the weight of sadness.

Self-care isn't indulgent. It's protection. It's how we pass on strength instead of sadness.

When you go through divorce, it's easy to end up at one extreme or the other, either being hurtful and reactive or trying so hard to protect your children that you block real emotional growth.

Divorce comes in many forms, but in most cases, one critical question remains: How far are you willing to go to hurt your ex because of your own pain? More importantly, how is that affecting your children? On the flip side, if you are dealing with an ex-partner trying everything to hurt you, what will you do to protect the children? Can you remain the stronger influence? Can you work to be proactive rather than reactive?

Too often, emotions take over, and people act out of

spite rather than thinking about the long-term conse-
quences. Would you rip phones out of the wall so your kids
can't reach their other parent? Block court-ordered visita-
tions, knowing it will drag them through legal battles? File
false claims to create obstacles?

Unless abuse is present, which is a different conversation entirely, these actions aren't about protecting your
children, they're about revenge.

If your ex is a decent parent outside of the pain they
may have caused you, they still deserve a relationship with
their children. The adult conflict should stay separate from
the parenting relationship.

What happens when children fight to maintain that
connection anyway? Maybe they're older, maybe they
understand far more than you realize. Do you punish them
too? Would you accuse them unfairly, or shame them for
wanting love and stability from both parents?

The key is finding that middle ground. I believe family therapy would have helped us find that balance much
sooner. Even with the best intentions, certain actions can
have long-term negative effects. When emotions like anger,
hurt, and confusion are running high, it's easy to make decisions that unintentionally harm the very people you want to
protect. Seeking help isn't just about personal healing.

Seeking help can be about creating stability and emotional safety for the children caught in the middle. There
are so many reasons for divorce, and every family's story is

different. That's why the delivery of every message to your children matters so much. Depending on the depth of your circumstances, you might need professional help to guide you through the process. One common mistake is using financial struggles as a weapon. Telling your children that their other parent isn't paying child support, or that you can't afford food or clothes because of them, only causes stress and fear.

Whether it's true or a spiteful exaggeration, it doesn't belong in your child's world. We had to deal with this ourselves, doing a lot of damage control over the lies that were told. Children should never have to carry those burdens. I also think about a close friend who faced one of the hardest challenges a parent can experience. She divorced her husband after finding out he had committed a crime and was sentenced to two years in prison. She was devastated. She had no idea he had been involved in anything illegal.

What amazed me was how she protected her children emotionally through it all. Instead of letting her anger spill into their hearts, she chose a different path. She didn't say, *Your dad is a terrible person.* She said, *Daddy made a mistake, and he's working hard to fix it.* She didn't lie; she was just careful. She knew that someday they would learn the truth, but she also knew it was her responsibility to protect their emotional security while they were still young.

With the help of a therapist, she was able to guide them through one of the most painful times without making it harder than it had to be. I've seen the other side too: parents who let their anger control them and destroy their children's ability to love freely. Remember that mother whose children, now adults, no longer speak to her? The pain she tried to inflict on her ex ended up costing her the very relationships she must have cherished most.

Children aren't blind. They sense emotional instability before they can name it. Once they do, it's hard to forget. They will feel manipulated. They will find their own truth, even when you try to hide it. (According to Psychology Today), studies show that almost 39% of children in high-conflict divorces show signs of PTSD. That's a heavy price to pay for unresolved pain. Taking care of yourself isn't a luxury, it's a necessity for you and your children. Healing yourself gives them a better chance at healing, too. Love, security, and emotional freedom come from the work you do inside your own heart.

If there's one thing I hope you take away from my story, it's that healing yourself is not separate from protecting your children. They are forever connected.

My wish for you and yours is that you continue doing the difficult work necessary to support your child's well-being and prevent incidents that could have lifelong effects.

xo,

Christina

JOURNAL MOMENT 11: Damage to Children

Only when you feel ready, sit with your journal, find a quiet space, and take time with these questions. You don't have to answer them all. Let them guide you toward what matters most right now, for you and your child. Take a moment to reflect. How will you get through this, with or without your partner? Some questions may not apply, or maybe you've already lived through them, but they can still help you write your story. When you're ready, make an entry in your journal.

State one or more ways you are currently caring for yourself.

Ask yourself: How far are you willing to go to hurt each other?

Are the children being put in the middle of it all?

Are your emotions clouding your ability to make mindful decisions that are in the best interest of your children?

List 1-5 ways you can improve this process for your children in the upcoming month.

Do the children see your emotions? Are they worried about you?

If your former spouse is causing this pain for the children, how can you support them? How can you work to not make it worse?

What are some of the things your children are dealing with and how can you support them?

You want to protect your children; reflect upon the many ways you can continue to do so, no matter what.

Are your plans in the best interest of the children?

Will you need professional guidance through this process?

What other ideas do you have from this reflection that you could journal?

Reflection Twelve:
Co-Parenting with Grace

PROMPT 12

Body scan meditation: This technique is ideal for this reflection because it encourages self-awareness and emotional regulation. If you are dealing with toxicity, whether from your ex, extended family, or your own emotions, a body scan can help identify and release physical tension linked to stress. It allows you to pause, reset, and ensure you aren't passing negativity onto your children. By regularly practicing this, you can approach parenting with more calmness and control, shielding your children from unnecessary emotional burdens.

THIS REFLECTION INVITES you to look ahead. What kind of relationship do you want to build with your children and former partner? Healing takes time; sometimes it takes months, sometimes it takes years. With steady effort and selflessness, it is possible to create something healthy, supportive, and real.

Our story ended in a beautiful place, but the path we took to get there was painfully hard. Hopefully, I have provided some tools along the way for you to get where you want to be.

One thing I always knew deep down was that Scott and I would keep parenting our daughter. We made that commitment the day she was conceived. I never thought we would continue parenting side by side all these years later. I knew he would show up for her, and I knew I would too, but I never imagined we would continue to do it together and so beautifully. There were so many unknowns, yet our parenting partnership grew into the friendship we share now.

I love that our daughter was the one who introduced us to the "bonus" concept instead of "step." Because she began calling her dad's wife her bonus mom, and my husband her bonus dad, I followed her lead and started calling Mike's kids my bonus kids. It feels more personal, more inclusive, and more loving.

That small shift created something closer between us all. "Bonus" made everyone feel included, not separate. "Step" felt distant, like someone on the outside. Our goal was always unity, and using the term "bonus" helped us live that. It made love feel bigger, not smaller.

Remember, it didn't begin that way. At first, Nichole called Tina her stepmom and Mike her stepdad. I called Mike's kids my stepkids. It felt distant at the time, but appropriate. We hadn't become a family yet. That took time, growth, patience, and open hearts . . . and still we got there.

I'll never forget that first Mother's Day when Nichole gave Tina a plaque with the definition of "Bonus mom." We both cried. It wasn't just a gift; it was a turning point. A moment of full-hearted acceptance that we could all feel and celebrate.

Another moment that stays with me is when Mike was promoted in the military. He told me he had a surprise. When you get promoted, the people who matter most to you punch your new rank onto your uniform. He chose his kids to do it, and he chose Nichole, too. That's how he sees her now. I'll never forget the look on her face. She was proud to join him on the stage in such a special moment. She felt included, and she knew she belonged.

For one of Nichole's birthdays, we rented a limo and went into Boston for dinner. Mike was there, and so were Scott, Tina, Nichole's boyfriend, my parents, and me. All of us together, celebrating. In 2022, we took a family trip to Scotland and Ireland. Later, we travelled to New Hampshire for my dad's 80th birthday. Again, all of us together.

Together, together, together.

There have been so many breakthrough moments along the way. Each one beautiful. Each one moving us closer to the family we are today. One unit, built through love, forgiveness, and the decision, repeatedly, to choose connection.

From left to right: Our daughter, our son-in-law, me, Mike, Tina, Scott in Scotland on a family trip 2022

TWO PARENTS FOR LIFE

Sometimes, after a divorce, one parent becomes the default—the one who takes the kids, the one who tucks them in every night—and the other parent becomes the one they miss. When that happens, especially with younger children, the sadness can run deep. I've seen it; I've felt it. Watching your child ache for someone they love is its own kind of heartbreak. So, if you're the parent they're with, what do you do?

You try to make it work. You try to find ways for them to spend more time with the other parent, not because it's easy, but because it's right. Think about it: When a child misses someone they love, they shouldn't have to face that ache in silence.

When Scott and I separated, we hoped we'd be able to come together again for birthdays, holidays, and milestones.

That first year, it became clear that without Nichole, we wouldn't have stayed in contact at all. We stayed connected for her. But over time, that thread became something stronger. Now we see each other more than we see Nichole. Somehow, we built a friendship we never thought possible.

Since we loved Nichole so much, and because we were committed to her safety and well-being, we never stopped being there. Over time, we started to change. We built a foundation of respect first, and then forgiveness. Time shifts everything, even when you think it won't. You might not see the path now, but growth comes, healing comes, and trust can be rebuilt.

If it's possible, hold onto the truth that your children deserve two parents for life. That commitment begins the day they are conceived and doesn't end when the marriage ends.

You keep showing up, even when it's hard, even if your ex won't meet you there. Your children need as many steady hands as possible, and for certain, they can have yours. Even if you're the only one trying, your children will notice. You can still build a future with them, one full of safety, love, and lasting memories.

I learned that when you focus on their well-being, when you protect them from the emotional fallout, you are still fulfilling your part of the parenting contract.

What we really wanted was to be strong enough to sit in

that stadium of life, to be the parents in the stands, always cheering our child on, no matter how messy the divorce had been. We wanted to protect her early adulthood, not let our pain define it.

Divorcing without children is very different from divorcing with children. Without kids, you can make decisions as adults, with only yourselves to consider. Maybe you stay friends, or maybe you part ways forever. In any case, when there are children involved, everything changes.

You must find a way to remain kind. You must protect their emotional safety above everything else.

There will be days when it feels impossible, days when it is hard to communicate without sending mixed signals or reopening old wounds. Yet somehow, you can keep pressing forward together—not perfectly, but with a shared purpose: protecting the children you both love more than anything.

Remember, you don't have to have it all figured out today. You are writing your family's story one choice at a time, and over time, the future you are building will take shape.

So, ask yourself:

- Where are you now?
- Are the people around you still broken, or have they started to heal?
- What does your family story look like next month, six months from now, one year from now?

Let's reconnect sometime over the next year. I would

love to hear more about the story you are writing.

PARENTING AFTER SEPARATION

The journey had its ups and downs, and nothing about it was simple. At first, Scott and I could show up to the same event, but we stayed on opposite sides of the room. Even sitting in the same row took time. We were trying, but if Nichole wasn't there, we didn't talk. We didn't cross paths unless we had to.

Eventually, after years had passed, the weight started to lift. Surprisingly, Tina and I became friends. That changed the shape of so much between us. It meant Scott and I were around each other more, and something in our dynamic began to shift. It was awkward at first. Over time, awkward gave way to something real.

When we were growing up, holidays were always separate, divided between families. We expected that would be our future too: seeing the kids separately, struggling to hold it all together. Even so, we worked hard to change that story.

When Scott and I divorced, I never thought we would get to where we are now. Like many ex-spouses, sometimes they can be stubborn, rigid, and not the most flexible person. Based on his reactions, I felt sure that was it. Nichole would always have to split her life between two very separate worlds. In time, we started building a foundation for something better. In those early days, neither of us could see a path forward.

Time changes things. Even if it feels impossible right now, you can grow too. Growth doesn't always happen fast, but it does come. You're shaping your story, even if the ending isn't clear yet. Whether you are like Scott and I and get to the amazing, blended family ending we did, OR facing a more difficult situation, find your way and do the work.

Sometimes, I'm asked if I think therapy is necessary. My answer is yes. Therapy can help you find common ground, even if it's not perfect. For my kids, I wanted to stay healthy and strong. I didn't want the divorces to take more from them than they already had. Therapy gave me tools to protect their peace and mine. Notice the shift from one divorce, one daughter to two divorces and multiple daughters and a son. My story has two sides, and we managed to blend them together in spite of all of the challenges.

I never imagined we would be where we are now. Traveling together, celebrating holidays together, truly a united family.

There's something beautiful about watching the walls fall away and rebuilding. About knowing that even though your story didn't follow the script you imagined, you built something real anyway.

If there's one thing I've learned, it's that not every story will look like mine and Scott's. Some stories will be harder, like Mike's. Some will take longer, and sometimes, no matter how much you want it, the other parent simply won't meet you halfway. Remember, you still have control. You can still choose to be the steady one, the safe one. The one your children will remember with gratitude.

Stay focused on what you can control: your actions, your words, your love for your children. Keep doing it the right way and seek support when you need it. Honor your parenting contract with your children. The rest will be what it will be, but *you* will always be able to feel good about *you*. Your kids will always be grateful to *you*.

What matters most is that your child knows you tried. You showed up; you led with love. Maybe your co-parent won't meet you halfway, and maybe they never will. In spite of it all, you can still choose to be steady, kind, and committed to doing what's best for your child. That's your part of the parenting contract.

Your kids may not understand it all right now. However, one day, they will. When they look back, they'll remember who stayed centered in love.

The important thing is that your children know you tried. *You stayed committed in what mattered most, even when it wasn't easy.* That's something no one can take away from you.

My wish for you and yours is that you can create a version of a healthy, cohesive relationship with your co-parent that will support the well-being of your child. If this is not possible in your story, I hope you find the peace you are seeking.

xo,

Christina

JOURNAL MOMENT 12: Your Future

Only when you feel ready, sit with your journal, find a quiet space, and take time with these questions. You don't have to answer them all. Just let them guide you toward what matters most right now, for you and your child. Take a moment to reflect: How will you get through this, with or without your partner? They may not all be relevant to your story, or maybe you've already been through these, but they will help you write it. When you're ready, make an entry in your journal.

Self-Reflection Prompts:

Take a moment to consider your long-term vision for your family's future. Ask yourself:

- How do I want my children to feel about both of their parents five or ten years from now?

- If my child were to describe their childhood, would they say I encouraged a healthy relationship with both parents or made their experience more difficult?

- What actions am I taking today that could have a lasting impact on my children's emotional well-being?

- If I remove my personal emotions from the situation, what is truly in the best interest of my child?

- What is one small step I can take this week to foster a more stable and supportive co-parenting dynamic?

State one or more ways you are currently caring for yourself.

Describe your current relationship with your former partner.

Is it where you want it to be?

What are some ideas you can work toward to make change?

What do you want your relationship to look like in a month, six months, one year, five years, 10 years from now?

Describe your current relationship with your children.

Are they feeling resentment, anger, uncertainties toward either of you? How can you support them?

If your former partner is unwilling to do the work with you, what can you do to encourage them, if anything?

Can you find some consistency together? Some way to co-exist for the children? Some way to show up for them?

If you remain alone in this, how will you press forward?

Do you feel like you have done absolutely everything you can to get your former partner to engage into the co-parenting model?

Are your plans in the best interest of the children?

Will you need professional guidance through this process?

What other ideas do you have from this reflection that you could journal?

Five Foundations for Protecting Your Child's Emotional Well-Being Through Divorce

1. UNDERSTAND THE LONG-TERM TRAJECTORY

- Divorce is a process, not a single event.
- Focus on evidence-based principles to support your child's emotional well-being.
- Express empathy and avoid harmful behaviors like labeling and blaming.

2. ENCOURAGE OPEN COMMUNICATION

- Use self-assessments and the 6 stages of change to understand emotional shifts.
- Create space for dialogue between parent and child: both short and in-depth conversations.
- Help children process their emotions in a healthy way.

3. PRIORITIZE EMOTIONAL AND SPIRITUAL WELL-BEING

- Practice breathing exercises and *The Prayer for Letting Go*.
- Recognize the difference between enabling and helping.

- Incorporate physical, emotional, and spiritual self-care into daily life.

4. MAINTAIN STABILITY AND BOUNDARIES

- Use the 3 AAA's chart: awareness, action, and acceptance.
- Identify what is robbing you of inner peace: what you are trying to control, struggling to let go of, or where you are lacking trust.
- Clarify your higher power and lean on personal growth.

5. FOSTER HEALING AND FORGIVENESS

- Reflect on what you appreciate and don't appreciate about your ex-partner.
- Work through the forgiveness chart: what they did, how it affected you, and whether you are ready to forgive.
- If you and your ex-partner can't get along, your child will feel forced to choose between you. Prioritize their well-being over personal conflict.

Messages to You, My Readers

– FROM THE REAL PEOPLE IN OUR STORY OUR LIVES –

THROUGHOUT THIS JOURNEY, the people you've read about, including my former husband, my current husband, my daughter, and our extended family, have all played a huge role in shaping the life we live today. They are more than just the characters in a story; they are my real friends and family, and they wanted to send you their own messages. These words come from their hearts as a way of sharing the love, healing, and hope we have all built together.

THIS IS OUR TODAY

Today, we are truly all together with my former husband and his wife, our daughter, my current husband, my bonus daughters, bonus granddaughter, and my bonus son. We celebrate together all the time, building wonderful memories. We cherish every moment and live a life of family and friendship.

FROM TINA: EMBRACING LOVE BEYOND DIVORCE: MY JOURNEY INTO A BLENDED FAMILY

When I met my husband, I wasn't just joining his life, I was stepping into a story that had already been written. He had a past, a former marriage, and most importantly, a daughter whose well-being depended on how we all chose to move forward. Blending into this family wouldn't be about erasing the past, but about embracing it with love, grace, and understanding.

At first, I wondered how I would fit into a dynamic that had already existed before me. Would there be tension? Resentment? Would I ever feel like a part of this family? These were natural fears, but I realized that the answer depended on my mindset. Instead of seeing his past as a threat, I chose to see it as a foundation, one that gave me the chance to be a part of growth *rather than* loss.

What made the difference was a shared commitment to keeping the family whole, even though its shape had changed. My husband's former wife and I had every reason to be wary of each other. But instead, we chose something radical: connection. We both had the desire to be part of each other's changing dynamic. We both wanted peace and believed in the same goal: to be part of a family that could thrive beyond divorce.

Of course, in the beginning, there were moments of discomfort and awkwardness, times when emotions ran high or misunderstandings arose. But I found that when I led with kindness instead of insecurity, and openness instead of being guarded, connections flourished. Over time, what started as a cautious coexistence became a genuine friendship, mutual respect, and a family dynamic that doesn't fit the conventional mold, but is filled with love.

Today, I don't just feel like my husband's wife in a blended family scenario; I feel like a part of something greater. I'm grateful to have his daughter as a very important part of my life, to have a relationship with her mother that is built on mutual respect, and to know that love isn't defined by the structure of a family, but by the heart we put into it.

In the end, by changing my perspective, I now have an amazing bonus daughter, a strong friendship with her mom, and an extended family that loves beyond measure. I will forever be grateful for everyone's part in co-creating this remarkable blended-family dynamic!

FROM MY PARENTS:

Dear readers,

We have known our son-in-law since he was 17 years old; he is like another son to us. When my daughter announced they were divorcing, we were devastated: *How is this going to work? We love our daughter so much, of course we will have to take her side. What about him? What about all the years we have loved him too? How are we going to get through this? How will we get our granddaughter through this?* We have seen far too many divorces and watched far too many people having to choose sides. We have witnessed many children suffer through divorce, so much separation, with family units crumbling to the ground. The fights, arguing, lawyers, court orders, years of horror. We didn't want to choose. How could we? Well, unlike most divorces, our daughter and son-in-law didn't make us choose. They took a less traditional approach, an approach that shocked everyone. To this day, it still shocks people. Our daughter didn't want us to stop loving our son-in-law. What was that going to solve? Nobody was going to benefit from the sabotage or revenge in divorce. She asked that we be patient with them both. She said that things would be hard for a while, but she always knew they would come back to some sort of friendship for our granddaughter. They both love her too much to make things hard on her. She knew it would be hard work, but she wasn't going to give up. I don't think any of us expected them to become what they have today.

If I can give you any advice after all we have seen in our lifetime, it would be to keep your children's best interests deep within your heart and soul. Keep working on your former partner if they cannot jump in with you. Beg if you must, but work hard to keep the children from the harmful lifetime effects a divorce can cause.

If you can find even a small amount of friendship to

continue co-parenting for your children, find it. They deserve the healthiest version of both of you. We wish you well.

FROM MIKE

Dear Readers

Going through my divorce was, without question, the most difficult experience of my life, even after enduring other significant traumas. I don't believe in preaching or overcomplicating things. I value honesty, simplicity, and relatability, and that's the spirit in which I offer this message.

I reached a point where I knew I could no longer stay in a marriage that wasn't healthy for any of us. As painful as it was, I realised that staying together was doing more harm than good, especially to our four young children. I had told myself I was staying for them, but over time, I saw they were suffering just as much as we were.

My divorce was, in many ways, a textbook example of how hard these situations can become. My ex-wife made every effort to alienate the children from me, involving them in legal and emotional battles they should never have had to witness. I was far from a perfect husband, but I have always strived to be a devoted father. Their well-being has always been my highest priority.

I told myself that if I focused on what was best for them, we would eventually come through the darkness. The journey was long—eighteen grueling months filled with challenges I wouldn't wish on anyone.

There were moments when the emotional strain felt unbearable. But in those times, I turned to my children. They became my anchor. Their needs gave me the strength to stay grounded.

In the end, I have all of my children, and we continue to strive. That outcome came from one guiding principle: I never lost sight of what was best for them. No matter the setbacks, no matter how many times I was knocked down, I kept going with their future in mind.

The most meaningful affirmation came later, when, separately, each of my children told me the same thing. Leaving the marriage was the right decision, and they were proud of me for it.

If you're reading this in a time of struggle, I hope this message and the book it accompanies offer you strength, clarity, and the tools to move forward. Even in the most painful situations, there is a way through. Sometimes, doing the hardest thing is exactly what's needed to protect the ones we love most.

Why I Wrote This Book

– MY PURPOSE –

FOR YEARS, I have been wanting to share our story with the world. It is a huge part of my journey to helping others. Everywhere we go together, we share our story. The reactions from people never get old. Choosing a different path certainly wasn't easy, but the rewards are now endless. Yes, the love and friendship we share are uncommon. In fact, most people think it is weird, like something is wrong with all of us. If people could truly understand how much this journey has shaped us all, I am confident that everyone would want a piece of the pie. But wait! Almost anyone can have this with hard work, dedication, trust building, and healing. My hope has always been that my book will help other couples find the strength to co-parent their children with grace. I hope you enjoyed this journey with me and will continue to do the work we discussed.

And always remember: *The children will be as good as you are.*

SHARED EXPERIENCES

There is so much we would have missed if we had followed the more traditional path. I can't imagine a life in which we weren't still together in some way, just because Scott and I ended our marriage. I think about all the divided moments Nichole could have faced. Who would she choose? Who would show up?

As a blended family, we've shared so many beautiful trips together over the years. In 2017, we went to Aruba. Then it was kayaking in Maine in 2019, a visit to Camden in 2021, and a dream trip to Scotland and Ireland in 2022. In 2023, we spent time in Turks and Caicos, followed by Bali in 2024. Our next adventure is already planned for 2025. Each journey has added another layer to the life we've built, full of shared memories and genuine connection.

From left to right: Me and Tina at my bachelorette celebration
2021

Me and Tina at the English Tea Room in Plymouth 2023

We have visited wineries, gone to Broadway shows, concerts, plays, and historical places. We have broken bread, made homemade wine, taken motorcycle rides, and walked beaches together. Tina and I share a tradition of looking for heart-shaped rocks, and we always seem to find them when we are together.

We've spent the last fifteen years celebrating birthdays together. When Mike proposed, Scott and Tina ended up being the very first people to know we were engaged. Before my parents, before Mike's Dad, even before our children, we told my ex-husband and his wife. That still makes me laugh. The waitress at the restaurant probably still tells the story, because she could not believe it.

For birthdays, we always come together. One year, we

had dinner at an upscale steakhouse in Boston for Scott's birthday. I love to cook and host as well. Mike's 40th was a huge event with over 200 guests. For my dad's 80th in New Hampshire, the whole family came together to celebrate.

This family is my support system. I believe we are one of the best examples of what a truly blended family can look like. We're connected in a real and lasting way.

We've created so many beautiful traditions. We go to spa days, attend The Boston Ballet every year, and catch local theatre shows and movie nights. We even do spontaneous outings, like our recent trip to see the second *Lion King* movie, *Mufasa*.

One of my favorite memories is the day we dressed up and went to an English tea shop in Plymouth. They served tea in delicate floral pots, with crumpets, finger sandwiches, and an incredible variety of blends to choose from. It felt like something out of a storybook, the four of us enjoying something simple and sweet together (my mom, me, Tina, and Nichole).

For Nichole's 21st birthday, five years after our divorce, we rented a limo that picked us up from my parents' house and took us into Boston for dinner at a beautiful Italian restaurant. It was one of those moments that reminded me how far we had come. We didn't just manage to coexist; we created joyful memories as a family.

When I think about what has held us together, it's not just one thing; it's longevity. It's deep friendships, filled with trust. It's everything we've been through and chosen to heal from. Over time, we've evolved as individuals and as a blended family, always keeping the children at the center.

As I write this chapter, I want to share what my most recent Mother's Day looked like. It was just a regular weekend in our blended family, but filled with more love than I know how to put into words. On Saturday morning, Tina and I met Nichole for a surprise she had planned. The three of us gathered at a local maritime center by the ocean. Nichole had gifted us a two-hour event where we shared snacks, did yoga, made flower arrangements, and sat down for coffee. The entire experience supported a local charity, which made it even more meaningful.

At the end, Nichole gave me a card, just like she always does, and that made me cry. In it, she wrote, "You are my number one, my rock, and my biggest supporter (tied with Dad). I really don't know how I got so lucky to have you as a mother. There is no one more selfless and caring than you. I cannot thank you enough for all that you do for me."

On Sunday morning, I woke up to flowers and a card from my bonus daughter that made me cry. The card reminded me how far we've come, how much our love has grown. She wrote, "I'm so lucky to have you around to share happy memories. Thank you for being such an incredible person for not just me, but all of us kids. We love you to the moon and back." Another moment that affirmed the reward of taking the high road and choosing to love, again and again.

Later that day, we went to my parents' house for lunch and yummy food. My bonus son handed me a plant and another beautiful card. He wrote, "Having you for a mom has been easily one of the best things in my entire life. I love you so much, and I am so proud to call you my mom." I cried again. How did I get so lucky? Every time I chose calm instead of conflict, every time I protected our peace, every heartache, every hard conversation. It all led to this, and it was worth it.

Mike gave me a card too. "To my wife. You are the girl I wanted from the start and the one I love with all my heart. Thank you for being the most amazing mom that my kids could ever ask for. I love you, sweetheart."

Then came a text from Scott, who wasn't feeling well that day. "Good morning. Happy Mother's Day to the best mom. I hope you have a wonderful day. Thank you for everything you do."

Tina, who joined us later that afternoon, also sent a message that morning. "I was just lying here thinking how much I love Nichole and wish she were my blood daughter, but then I thought, *Well, then she wouldn't be your daughter and I wouldn't have you.* Anyway, just wanted to share my morning gratitude. Happy Mother's Day."

This is us. This is our life now. This weekend is just one small glimpse of the many memories we've created and continue to create: all of us, together.

From left to right: my bonus daughter and me out for an impromptu dinner on the water 2023

We even share the same travel bucket list. The best part? We never fight on vacations. It just works. Best traveling buddies ever! The upcoming trip is going to be a very special one because we are celebrating two special milestone birthdays together.

Many of the friends who watched our divorce unfold have now embraced the friendship Tina and I built. Some of them have even said they believe Scott and I were meant to move on so that Tina and I could meet. That thought still touches me. Tina is more than my friend; she's my soul-sister, my kindred spirit. Our relationship has brought so much joy and healing to everyone around us.

When we go out together, we still get looks. We tell our story to strangers, and their reactions are priceless. "We're

From left to right: my bonus son and me at St. Anthony's Feast in Boston-our annual tradition 2022

going out with my ex-husband and his wife," I'll say. They always blink twice. "Wait, what? You're all friends?" They're amazed. Inspired, even.

Nichole embraces it too. She searches for gifts that say *bonus mom and bonus dad*. She posts about all of us on Facebook. She knows this is special. That we built something most people don't even think is possible.

Mike and Scott are great friends, too. They go out on the Harleys together, golf, meet for lunch, and talk when they need a friend. It warms my heart to watch my former husband and my current husband share such a caring relationship. After all, how many people can truly say that!

Looking back, I can't imagine my life without Tina, or without the bonds we've all formed: me, Scott, Tina, and

Mike. We are a team; we've created a new kind of family. A family that has expanded and evolved beyond anything I could have ever pictured. Maybe the most surprising part is this: it doesn't even have to revolve around Nichole anymore. We're just us. A friendship built on love, trust, and respect.

Conclusion

MORE THAN ANYTHING, I hope this book reaches the people who need it most. I wrote it to remind anyone going through divorce that healing is possible. Even when everything feels broken, there is still a way forward. If Scott and I could create a new kind of family after everything we faced, maybe others can too. Not because it's easy, but because it's worth it. For your children, for the people who love you, and for yourself.

There is no perfect way to navigate divorce, but there is a thoughtful way through it. It begins with self-reflection. It is not about getting everything right or becoming best friends with your ex. It is about showing up, again and again, with your child's well-being at the center.

Ask yourself gently: Am I hurting my child in this process? Am I making space for their love to remain whole, even if mine has changed?

You are not divorcing your children. You are divorcing each other. That difference matters. How you handle that choice shapes your family's emotional future.

You don't need to aim for perfection. Just keep choosing presence over punishment, reflection over reaction, and love over control. Be kind to yourself; be kind to them. That's the work. To raise a generation that doesn't have to recover from how we handled our pain.

The day I walked out the door, we felt hatred, pain, and emotions we thought we might never recover from. Today, we still say I love you. It just means something different now.

We've found real joy in each other's company. As a group, we're living life more fully. I believe the universe sets our pathways, and everything that's happened has made us stronger, more evolved, and more connected.

I got through it without tools. *Just my mind, my body, and my spirit carried me.*

I survived; we survived. I learned that even when you feel broken beyond repair, something greater can still hold you up.

You can get through it, too.

Love,

Christina

xo

Special Thanks to...

Our daughter for being so easy to love and keeping us on the path.

God, for your guidance.

My parents, for always believing in me and teaching me to believe in myself.

Our blended family, for standing by each other through the hardest times and building a beautiful life together.

Bali, for the experience, the connections, the inspiration, and the creativity it sparked.

Let's Stay Connected

Visit **bhplove.com** to join the
Building Healthy Pathways community.

Follow me on Facebook:
Facebook.com/buildinghealthypathways/

Follow me on Instagram:
@building_healthy_pathways

*Sign up for the email list to access forums,
educational seminars, wellness and nutrition tips,
and podcast updates. Most importantly, I would
love to hear about your journey. I look forward to
staying connected with you!*

www.ingramcontent.com/pod-product-compliance
Lightning Source LLC
Chambersburg PA
CBHW071723120626
46550CB00001B/354